D0801491

DISCARD

THE CHICAGO PUBLIC LIBRARY

FORM 19

"BRIAN'S SONG"
ABC-TV "Movie of the Week"

Producer: Paul Junger Witt
Director: Buzz Kulik
Screenplay by: William Blinn
Music by: Michel Legrand

Starring
James Caan as Brian Piccolo
Billy Dee Williams as Gale Sayers
and Jack Warden as Coach Halas
Shelley Fabares as Joy Piccolo
Judy Pace as Linda Sayers

Produced by
SCREEN GEMS

George Foster Peabody Award
Directors Guild of America Award
Writers Guild of America Award
Golden Globe Award nomination
Golden Reel Award nomination

"Eddie" nomination by the American Cinema Editors

National Conference of Christians and Jews
the Mass Media Brotherhood Award "For
Outstanding Contributions to Better Human Relations
and the Cause of Brotherhood."

Black Sports Magazine Award "For Interracial
Understanding Through the Medium of Sports."

Congressional Record commendation as "one of
the truly moving television and screen
achievements in recent years."

American Cancer Society Special Citation

NAACP commendation

BRIAN'S SONG

SCREENPLAY

BY WILLIAM BLINN

BANTAM BOOKS
TORONTO • NEW YORK • LONDON • SYDNEY • AUCKLAND

PN
1997
.B729
B5
1972b
R00648 77524

RL 6, IL age 12 and up

BRIAN'S SONG
A Bantam Book / September 1972
29 printings through September 1983

All rights reserved.
Copyright © 1972 by Columbia Pictures Industries, Inc.
This book may not be reproduced in whole or in part, by
mimeograph or any other means, without permission.
For information address: Bantam Books, Inc.

Library of Congress Cataloging in Publishing Data

Blinn, William.
    Brian's song.

1. Piccolo, Brian, 1943-1970—Drama 2. Sayers, Gale, 1943-
—Drama 1. Brian's song (Motion picture) II. Title.
PN1997.B729B5   812'.5'4   72-5235

ISBN 0-553-24072-2

Published simultaneously in the United States and Canada

Bantam Books are published by Bantam Books, Inc. Its trade-
mark, consisting of the words "Bantam Books" and the por-
trayal of a rooster, is Registered in U.S. Patent and Trademark
Office and in other countries. Marca Registrada. Bantam
Books, Inc., 666 Fifth Avenue, New York, New York 10103.

PRINTED IN THE UNITED STATES OF AMERICA

H   38 37 36 35 34 33

BRIAN'S SONG

FADE IN:

EXTERIOR—ROLLING COUNTRYSIDE—
DAY (HELICOPTER SHOT)

The terrain is farmland, flat, tranquil, soothing in its simplicity. As our view gets closer to the ground, we start to hear the Narrator's voice, and it wouldn't hurt if that voice belonged to Don Meredith.

> NARRATOR (*Voice Over*)
> This is a story about two men, one
> named Gale Sayers, the other Brian
> Piccolo. They came from different
> parts of the country. They competed
> for the same job. One was white;
> the other black. One liked to talk;
> the other was as shy as a three-year-
> old. Our story's about how they
> came to know each other, fight each
> other, and help each other . . .
> (*beat*)
> Ernest Hemingway said that every
> true story ends in death. Well,
> this *is* a true story.

As the helicopter continues its descent, we now find ourselves following a car as it makes its way down a two-lane asphalt road. Coming closer, we note the color and dome roof light that identify it as a cab. We follow the cab as we roll opening credits.

DIRECT CUT TO:

EXTERIOR—CAMPUS-TYPE AREA—DAY—
ON SIGN

Reading: "Training Camp of the Chicago Bears," an NFL insignia beneath the lettering. We pan off the sign, moving by a number of red brick buildings, the kind of ivied architecture seen at any number of small universities in the Middle West. Coming up the curving blacktopped drive is the cab.

EXTERIOR—PRACTICE FIELD—
SERIES OF CUTS

The Bears are going through the various routines and exercises. Defensive linemen scuttling crablike back and forth as a coach switches a ball from hand to hand. Men working on the blocking shed, throwing their bulk against the padded metal arm. Players negotiating the rope framework, some alternating, crossing over, others hopping from square to square. Throughout these cuts, the sounds of men under strain, struggling for breath, grunting with effort as they bear down.

TIGHT ON FOOTBALL

Teed up for a place-kick. It is booted out of frame, the kicker's foot no more than a swift blur as we zoom toward the far end of the field, where we can see Gale Sayers standing by the driver's side of the cab, his suitcase next to him, writing on the cabdriver's clipboard.

Sayers is in his early twenties, his handsome face normally enigmatic, guarded. He's dressed in slacks and sport coat, but even in this kind of "civilian" garb, it doesn't take a practiced eye to note the lean, hard compactness of a born athlete.

CLOSER ANGLE—GALE AND CABDRIVER

Gale pays the cabdriver.

> BRIAN (*Voice Over*)
> Heads up! Look out!

Gale looks toward the sound of the voice just in time to react to the football hurtling down toward him. He gets a hand up and slaps it away, over the cab. The driver shoots an unfriendly look toward the field as he drops the car into gear and drives off. Gale walks across to the other side of the road to get the football.

DIFFERENT ANGLE

Gale turns to throw the ball to the young man now approaching him. He's wearing a Bears' sweat shirt, workout shorts, football cleats. This is Brian Piccolo— early twenties, with a smile that comes easily and nicely, though it's not something he ever "uses." He takes life and people as he finds them, and he generally finds them worthwhile, enjoyable, and a little funny. The face is strong and handsome, an accurate reflection of the man's makeup. Gale throws the ball back across the road to him.

GALE

Here you go.

BRIAN

Thanks.

He turns and heaves the ball back to the practice area offstage, though he makes no move to return there himself. Gale goes to his suitcase, a little ill at ease when Brian just stands there looking at him with a half smile.

BRIAN

You're Gale Sayers.

GALE

Yeah.

BRIAN

I'm Brian Piccolo. We met at the
All-America game last June in Buffalo.

Brian has extended his hand, but Gale is holding his suitcase. A short beat as Gale switches hands, but by the time it's done, Brian has taken back his hand, and there's one of those social situations of stuttering reactions. Finally, they shake hands. Gale's head is down, face guarded.

GALE

Sorry I didn't remember, but I'm
not very good at that kind of stuff.

Piccolo's smile is a nice one.

BRIAN

(*a quiet put-on*)
Golly, that's okay. I can see why

you might forget, but I sure
couldn't. No way. That was a
heckuva talk we had, man. I mean,
I walked up and said: "I'm Brian
Piccolo. I hear we'll both be
playing for the Bears." And you
said—I'll never forget it—you
said: "Uh-huh." Just like that.
"Uh-huh." And whenever I'm feeling
depressed or low, why, I think about
that advice. Lot of guys wouldn't
have taken the time to talk to me
like that, but not you. "Uh-huh,"
you said. Just like that. Right
out.

Brian grins. Gale does not. His expression is neutral.
A short beat.

GALE

Where do I go to check in?

Piccolo's smile goes. The total lack of reaction from
Gale is puzzling. He nods toward one of the buildings
offstage.

BRIAN

That building over there. That's
where Halas is.

GALE

Thanks.

The word comes in a characteristic flat tone. Gale
moves off for the building. Brian stands there a moment,
looking after him thoughtfully.

BRIAN

Hey . . .

Gale stops, looking back.

GALE

What?

BRIAN

You ever met Halas before?

GALE

Talked to him on the phone a couple times. That's all.

Brian's manner is calm, pleasant, helpful.

BRIAN

Well, look, let me give you a little hint. He's a good guy and all, but he's deaf in his left ear and he's too vain to admit it. So stay on his right-hand side, or he won't hear a word you say. .

GALE

(*beat*)
Uh—okay. Thanks.

BRIAN

Rookies have to stick together, man.

With a wave of his hand, Brian starts off, moving at an easy lope back onto the practice field. Sayers stands there, watching Brian, not knowing precisely what to make of him. After a moment, he turns and starts for the building pointed out by Piccolo.

DIRECT CUT TO:

INTERIOR—BEARS' MAIN OFFICE CORRIDOR—
DAY—FULL SHOT

The look of the corridor is that of a high school or small
college.

ANGLE ON GALE

He comes in looking about uneasily, then heads for the
end of the corridor.

HIS POINT OF VIEW—ON DOOR—
MOVING SHOT

Pushing in to the nameplate on the door reading:
Coach George Halas.

FULL SHOT

As Gale stops in front of the door, he wipes his sweat-
ing palms on his trouser legs, then knocks on the
door.

> HALAS
> (*impatiently, offstage*)
> Yeah. Come in.

Gale stands motionless for a second, gathering his
forces, then opens the door and steps inside.

INTERIOR—HALAS'S OFFICE—DAY—
ANGLE ON GALE

As he comes into the office, looking offstage, he starts
to speak, but his voice is elsewhere, only a dry croak.

FULL SHOT

The office is in a state of organized chaos. Cardboard

filing boxes, cartons of books and papers. Reels of 16mm film and, standing behind the ancient desk, a large man of some years, some strength and much power: Halas. He holds a framed picture, hammer, and nails, apparently involved in finding just the right place for it. He looks at the young man standing in the doorway.

HALAS

I'm George Halas.

GALE

I know.
  (*quickly*)
I mean, everyone knows who you
are. I'm Gale Sayers.

HALAS

Come on in, Gale. You can give me
a hand hanging this thing. My good
luck picture. First professional
team I ever played on. The Decatur
Staleys in 1920.

Gale steps in, closing the door, still in awe and afraid. Halas moves to an empty place on the wall, his back to Gale.

HALAS

How's your leg? I read where it
was hurt.

GALE

It's fine. Hundred percent.

HALAS

How about your head?

GALE

My head? Nothin' wrong with my head.

HALAS

Good. Because being in the All-Star
game puts you three weeks behind
everybody else. New terminology,
new plays to learn. Won't be easy.

GALE

(*beat*)
NFL ain't supposed to be easy.

A smile and look from Halas. He nods.

HALAS

Right. Give me a hand.

Gale moves behind the desk, where Halas is holding
the picture up against the wall. Gale takes over, allow-
ing Halas to start hammering a nail to hold the picture.

HALAS

About all I can promise you is a
fair shot at running back. But
you're going to have a lot of com-
pany. Jon Arnett, Ralph Kurek,
Brian Piccolo . . . going to be very
crowded out there.

Gale looks at Halas for a second, realizing he's on the
man's left side, recalling the advice given him by Brian

earlier. Still holding the picture, he rumbas around behind and then to the other side of the Coach.

GALE

Well, a fair shot is all I want.
Can't ask for more than that.

Halas notes Gale's shift with a puzzled look, then drives the nail home. He turns back to the desk, once more placing Gale on his left side.

HALAS

We plan to use our backs a good deal
as receivers this year. You do much
pass catching when you were in college?

He looks back to where Gale was, only to find that Gale has crossed behind him to the good side.

GALE

Well, yes sir, I did, but it was
usually safety-valve stuff. Once
in awhile we'd screen.

Halas spots an envelope out of place on the desk. He picks it up and moves to one of the filing cabinets nearby. He opens the drawer and puts the envelope in.

HALAS

Well, I generally prefer to get a
back into the pattern, unless the
other team has a tendency to blitz.
That's another thing you'll have to
get used to, checking out the line-
backers, make sure they aren't coming.

Halas looks back to Gale, but once again, he's the

man who isn't there. Gale has managed to cross behind him again, squeezing in between Halas and the wall, struggling to make the move seem ever so casual.

GALE

Yes sir, I know . . .

Halas starts back to the desk, once again forcing Gale to do an end around.

GALE

. . . and, especially on teams like the Cardinals, I guess . . .

HALAS

(*exasperated*)
Damn it, Sayers—what's the matter with you?

GALE

I—I don't know what you mean . . .

HALAS

I know you've got moves, but you don't have to show them to me now! You're hopping around here like a pauper in a pay toilet!

GALE

(*sputtering*)
Well, I—I was just trying to stay on the side with your good ear . . .

HALAS

Good ear? What are you talking about, good ear?

GALE

Well, Brian Piccolo told me that—
he said—uh—he—uh . . .

Halas waits for the sentence to end, but it's not going
to. For the realization is slowly dawning on Gale that
he has been had. He mulls telling Halas, but that's
only going to make him look sillier. Gale struggles to
manufacture a smile as Halas stares at him.

DIRECT CUT TO:

INTERIOR—DINING HALL—NIGHT—
ANGLE ON STEAM TABLE

The table is piled with food, the piles being assaulted
by a number of large men, who ladle on portions that
would choke a disposal. Thick necks, massive frames,
moving with the laconic, easy confidence of a jock.
At a centrally placed table, we can see Halas, his
coaches and key players.

CLOSER ANGLE—COACHES' TABLE

Seated on one side of Halas is Ed McCaskey, a handsome man in his early fifties. On the other side is
Abe Gibron, a man who is all football; Sophia Loren
in a zebra-striped bikini would remind him of a ref-
eree. One man at the table is standing. This is J. C.
Caroline, a man in his late twenties, tall and lean,
built for speed. He has a packet of three-by-five index
cards he consults as he speaks.

CAROLINE

Some of you guys who pulled in today

haven't had a chance to hear what's
going to be expected of you, so pipe
down for a little bit, let me talk.

ANGLE ON GALE

He is seated at one of the rear tables, exchanging
"pass-the-salt" conversations with the other men nearby, all of whom are black. The man next to Gale
finishes his plate and vacates the chair as Caroline
continues to speak offstage. Gale reacts with an inward
"damn" as Brian Piccolo approaches and starts to un-
load his tray in the place next to Gale. Gale tries to
hide his displeasure at the spot Piccolo has chosen.

As Piccolo starts to eat, Caroline drones on offstage.

CAROLINE

(*continuing offstage*)
You new guys are going to be given a
playbook tomorrow. It's like the Bible,
except the Gideons don't replace it for
free. Neither do the Bears. Lose the
playbook and the fine is five hundred
dollars. No exceptions, no appeal.
Five–double–o. Second thing is
curfew. You don't like it; I don't
like it. Well, that's just tough
sleddin', because that fine is ten
bucks for every fifteen minutes and
there's no appeal from that either,
so I hope she's worth it if you get the
yen. . . . Now—for talking in team
meeting . . .

Caroline starts to become aware of Gale and Brian speaking offstage.

> **BRIAN**
>
> Sayers, we can't go on meeting like this—my wife's getting suspicious.

> **GALE**
>
> Buzz off. I'm trying to listen to the Man.

> **BRIAN**
>
> No need, no need. I've been through this lecture twice already. If you lose the playbook, a fine of five big ones. Lose the playbook a second time, and they cut off your foot and feed it to the defensive platoon.

> **GALE**
>
> Just cool it, would you, please?

> **BRIAN**
>
> Just trying to be helpful.

> **GALE**
>
> Yes—like you "helped" me with Halas. Well, I don't need your kind of . . .

> **CAROLINE**
> (*loudly offstage*)
> *Mister* Sayers!

WIDER ANGLE

J. C. Caroline fixes Gale with the look that's chilled

any number of feckless flankers. Every eye in the room is on Gale, and most are relishing his pained reaction.

> CAROLINE
> (*continuing*)
> I was mentioning the fine for talking in a team meeting. Did you happen to hear me?

> GALE
> No, I did not.

> CAROLINE
> The fine is twenty-five dollars, Mister Sayers. And it's just been levied on you, *dig?*

> GALE
> (*seething*)
> Yeah.

ANGLE ON GALE AND BRIAN

Piccolo stares straight ahead, lips trembling as he tries to mask the laughter building up within him.

> BRIAN
> (*sotto*)
> Sorry, man . . .

Gale glares at him, homicide in mind. Slow homicide.

ANGLE TO CAROLINE AND HALAS

Halas leans over and nods toward the table where Gale and Brian are seated. A few words from Halas, and Caroline nods agreement.

FULL SHOT

Caroline gets to his feet, tapping the water glass once again for attention.

>   **CAROLINE**
> It's been brought to my attention
> that unless Sayers was saying his
> beads it might be fair if Mr.
> Piccolo was to give us a little
> song. Say—a fight song. Wake
> Forest, wasn't it, Mr. Piccolo?

ANGLE TO BRIAN AND GALE

Gale's look acknowledges that there may be some justice in this old world after all. To his surprise, however, the singing gauntlet troubles Brian not at all. He smiles, rising, and when he sees the surprise on Gale's face, leans over to whisper.

>   **BRIAN**
> Can't let it get to you, man—
> it's all a question of *style*.
> Style, I say . . .

He is up on the chair, launching into the Wake Forest fight song, giving it a rousing tempo, and booming volume. Brian thrives on this kind of thing; you can't force-feed sugar to an ant.

TIGHT ON GALE

No, there isn't any justice, after all. Brian continues singing offstage, and Gale broods upon the inequities of this life. Then, deliverance—his eye falls on something offstage in the direction of Brian's plate.

HIS POINT OF VIEW—THE PLATE

Shot is centered on two mammoth dollops of mashed potatoes swimming in rich brown gravy. Steaming and gloppy.

ANGLE ON GALE

He takes a spoon and fork, glancing up to make sure Brian is still concentrating on the song, then moves to transfer the potatoes to the seat of Brian's chair.

ANGLE ON BRIAN

Al Martino, look to your laurels. He even goes into a trombone imitation as he nears the big finish.

WIDER ANGLE

Gale has another big finish to contemplate and he greets the end of the Wake Forest fight song with polite applause. Brian waves a cordial hand to those clapping, then hops down lightly and sits—without looking. Gale just sits there, looking at Brian, enjoying the rush of expressions that go rolling across his face. Disbelief. Dread. Realization. A look to the absent mashed potatoes on his plate. Acceptance. By the time he slowly swings his look over to Gale, the young black man is just getting to his feet, face composed. Before he goes, however, he reminds Brian.

GALE

It's all a question of style—
style, I say . . .

He moves off, camera closing on Piccolo. He turns squishily, watching Gale saunter off. He can't quite work up a smile, but neither can he get to a point of being very angry about it. He can take it as well as hand it out, it seems.

DIRECT CUT TO:

EXTERIOR—PRACTICE FIELD—DAY—
TIGHT ON GIBRON

Abe Gibron is an assistant coach possessed of a voice that could shatter a glass eye at fifty paces when the eyelid is closed. When we pull back, we will see that Gibron is presently riding herd on a number of offensive backs, Sayers and Piccolo in the forefront, as they lower their heads and dig against the resistance of the harness looped about their shoulders and fastened to a stone wall. Gibron will not be happy until one of the men pulls down the wall.

GIBRON
Dig! Dig! Dig! Come on! What's
wrong with you? You're not trying!
You're not trying! You make me
sick! Dig—dig—dig!

HARD CUT TO:

EXTERIOR—PRACTICE FIELD—DAY—
FULL SHOT

Fifty men hit the dirt at gut-rending impact, then are up on their feet, running in place—huge men, human trees, gasping for breath, posture deteriorating—then damn! down! and it hurts, that's the only word, and they're up and running once more, knees pistoning clods of earth.

                              HARD CUT TO:

EXTERIOR—PLAYING FIELD—DAY—
TIGHT ON GIBRON

Martin Bormann is not in Argentina.

                        GIBRON
     Mark! Set! Go!

FULL SHOT—OFFENSIVE BACKS—FAVORING

Sayers and Piccolo come out of a sprinter's crouch, taking each other on in wind sprints, their faces locked with drive and desire.

ANGLE TO THE FORTY-YARD LINE

Halas and a number of other coaches are standing. Gale tears across the line a full stride ahead of the others. Stopwatches are held out for Halas's perusal. He notes the results and is pleased.

ANGLE ON GALE AND BRIAN

They draw up, both sagging, leaning forward, hands on knees as they try to pull more air in. This may be the tenth wind sprint they've run today. Between gasps of breath:

                        BRIAN
     Well—I think it's working.

                        GALE
     What's working?

BRIAN

I'm getting you overconfident.

HARD CUT TO:

INTERIOR—TEAM MEETING ROOM—DAY— ON BLACKBOARD

A play is diagramed on the blackboard, the area covered with circles and Xs, dotted lines and arrows. Halas is the man with the chalk. No need to hear what he's saying—his look and the manner in which he raps the chalk against the slate get the message across.

ANGLE ON SAYERS AND PICCOLO

They are seated near the front with the rest of the players, all of whom are studying the board as if their lives depended on it. Which, in one sense, it does. The look of exhaustion is shared by all as they listen and frantically scribble notes.

DIRECT CUT TO:

EXTERIOR—PRACTICE FIELD—DAY— FULL SHOT

Offensive backs are going one-on-one with members of the defensive unit: an alley marked off of no more than eight or ten feet in which to maneuver. Sayers is first off the line and a second later, the defensive man is sprawled in the dirt thinking of life with the Montreal Alouettes. We zoom past the man to Piccolo, a few places back in the offensive backfield line; he's impressed, and a little afraid.

DIRECT CUT TO:

EXTERIOR—PRACTICE FIELD—DAY—
FULL SHOT

The offense and defense take measure of one another.
They line up, the ball is snapped. There is a brief
flurry of motion, then the quarterback is embraced
and downed by a large man from the defensive unit.
As they all untangle themselves to the accompaniment
of the whistles, Brian gets up and finds himself being
glared at by Abe Gibron.

GIBRON
Pic! You boneheaded wop! That
was a fake draw, screen right!
What's your assignment on a fake
draw, screen right?

BRIAN
My assignment on a fake draw,
screen right, is to pick up the
linebacker, if he's coming, unless
the linebacker is Dick Butkus.
Then I simply notify the quarterback
and send for a priest.

Laughter from the others on this, which only serves to
further enrage Gibron.

ANGLE ON GALE

He is smiling broadly at Piccolo's reply—smiling, perhaps, in spite of himself.

GIBRON (*Offstage*)
Come on, you guys, don't! You
just encourage him, that's all!
Knock it off!

DIRECT CUT TO:

EXTERIOR—PRACTICE FIELD—NIGHT—
FULL SHOT

Gale moves along the walk bordering the practice
area dressed in casual sports clothes, an afterdinner
stroll. He nears us, then stops, looking offstage, expression
puzzled.

HIS POINT OF VIEW—ON BRIAN

In the middle of the empty practice field, he falls into
a three-point stance, counts off a whispered cadence
of signals, then breaks to his right. Just as he's about
to turn upfield, he brakes sharply and cocks his arm,
letting an imaginary pass go. Apparently, the imaginary
receiver caught the ball, because Piccolo's expression
is pleased as he turns back—and sees Gale
watching his pantomime. He shugs.

BRIAN
I'm dynamite until there's someone
playing against me.

ANOTHER ANGLE

Gale moves to him, still a little puzzled.

BRIAN
Practicing the halfback option.
I'm not too good at it, and it

looks as if they want to use it
a lot.

GALE

(*politely*)
Oh, you'll get the hang of it.

Brian smiles, sitting on the grass.

BRIAN

Wish I was as sure of that as you
are. Tell you the truth, Sayers
—I envy you.

GALE

How come?

BRIAN

Because they've got a lot of
money tied up in you. They can't
cut you.

Gale just looks at him for a second, then turns abruptly
and starts off. Piccolo groans, falling back on the grass
with exasperation. He calls after Gale.

BRIAN

(*simply*)
And you're too good to get cut,
bonus or no bonus.

Gale stops, turns back slowly.

BRIAN

(*beat*)
And I'm too good, too, but I'm
not sure I've proved that to
the Old Man yet.

Gale is thrown off stride mentally. Piccolo's easy direct-ness takes some getting used to. Brian views him with a small smile.

> BRIAN
>
> Sayers—I am bending over back-
> wards to get through that turtle
> shell of yours. Can't you at
> least say thank you or something?

> GALE
>
> Well—I don't do things like you
> do—telling jokes and all that
> kind of—you know—I—I'm more
> of a . . .
> 　(*considers*)
> Thanks.

A quick nod, then Gale turns and heads back in the direction of the dormitory. Piccolo smiles, taking even this small breakthrough as some kind of progress. He gets to his feet and is about to go through the half-back option once more.

> GALE (*Offstage*)
> Hey, Piccolo?

FULL SHOT

Gale has stopped at the walk. Brian straightens up.

> BRIAN
> Yeah?

Gale glances at the ground; he'd rather send a letter.

GALE

Try it going to your left. They
don't look for a right-handed
guy to throw going to his left.

Brian nods, smiling as their eyes meet; Gale's look still
a guarded one.

BRIAN

(*beat*)
Thanks.

TIGHT ON GALE

He shrugs, glances down.

GALE

Well, like you said—us rookies
got to stick together.

HARD CUT TO:

INTERIOR—HALLWAY OUTSIDE HALAS'S
OFFICE—DAY—ON DOOR

Gale raps on the door several times.

HALAS (*Offstage*)
Come on in, Gale.

Gale opens the door and steps in, camera following to
reveal Halas behind the desk, Ed McCaskey seated
nearby, and J. C. Caroline doodling on the blackboard
that bears the serpentine diagrams of plays and pat-
terns. Gale views the three with a mixture of fear and
curiosity.

HALAS
You know Ed McCaskey, don't you,
Gale? And J.C.?

Affirmative ad-libs come from Gale and the other two
men. Gale takes the chair that has obviously been left
vacant for him. Halas nods toward a pitcher of iced
tea resting in front of him.

HALAS
Want some iced tea?

GALE
Uh, yeah. Please.

Halas pours him a glass, the cubes tinkling. Gale
fidgets, well aware of Caroline and McCaskey watching him. Halas hands him the glass.

HALAS
Tell you what we wanted to talk
to you about, Gale. . . . See, I'm
an old-timer in a lot of ways . . .
    (*a look to Caroline
    and McCaskey*)
At least that's what people keep
telling me—but I don't think it's
all that uncommon for a man my age
to get used to the way things are—
to be comfortable with things. You
understand what I'm saying?

GALE
    (*baffled*)
I guess so . . .

HALAS

Well, what it comes down to is
that J.C. here had a notion and
he talked to Ed about it, and Ed
thinks it's a good idea—and I
guess maybe it's time for some
changes around here. You follow
me?

GALE

You want me to play flanker, not
running back.

The other three exchange a smile at this, but Gale's
still flying blind.

MC CASKEY

Not that simple, Gale. J.C.'s
point—and one I agree with—
is that it's 1965 and it's time
the Bears roomed together by
position—without any regard to
race.

CAROLINE

We'd like you and Brian Piccolo
to room together.

Gale smiles; he was at three hundred feet and the
chute finally opened.

GALE

Is that all? Is that what this
is about?

CAROLINE

Is that all?

GALE
Yeah. You had me worried. I
thought it was something really . . .

TIGHT ON CAROLINE

His index finger shoots out, pinning Gale to the chair.

CAROLINE
Sayers—this *is* something, really.
This is a white man and a black man
rooming together on a team where
that's never been done before. You're
going to be called a Tom by some
blacks and an uppity nigger by some
whites. And when we go on the road,
we'll be going to Atlanta and Dallas
and Houston and Miami—and don't
think it's going to get any better in
Los Angeles and Detroit and Chicago,
and every other town we play in, 'cause
it *won't*.
    (*beat*)
You're going to rock the boat, Sayers—
and there's plenty of people around
who are already seasick.

FULL SHOT

A beat, as Caroline holds Gale's gaze, then straightens
up. Halas has a small smile on his face.

HALAS
Have a glass of iced tea, J.C.

Caroline does so, smiling a little sheepishly, as well. Halas leans forward.

> **HALAS**
> What J.C. is saying is that there
> may be pressures, Gale. Severe
> ones.
> (*simply*)
> Now! What do *you* say?

ANOTHER ANGLE—ON GALE

Recovering from Caroline's onslaught, he takes a breath, looking beyond the three men, giving the question the steady introspection it deserves.

DIRECT CUT TO:

INTERIOR—DORMITORY HALLWAY—
NIGHT—ON BRIAN

He comes down the hallway, wearing a windbreaker and casual slacks, offstage we can hear the sound of muted rock music. Brian's face is set, dour and depressed. He stops in front of one of the doors, pulls a key out of his pocket, then registers: that music is coming from his room. He looks down at the space between the door and the floor. There's light peeping out from within the room. Puzzled, he puts the key in the lock and opens the door cautiously.

INTERIOR—THE ROOM—ON BRIAN

He swings the door open and looks in, still baffled by what he sees.

BRIAN'S POINT OF VIEW— ON BULLETIN BOARD

There is a picture thumbtacked to the bulletin board, the image there of Joy Piccolo and a small baby girl. We pan over to reveal another picture tacked up on the bulletin board next to Joy's. The second picture is of Linda Sayers. We pan down from this picture to find Gale sprawled out on the bed, the radio blaring by his side. He reaches out and turns off the radio.

GALE

Hi. We're rooming together.

FULL SHOT

Brian steps into the room and closes the door as though stepping through the Looking Glass. He looks at Gale evenly.

BRIAN

Says who?

GALE

Who else?

BRIAN

(*sourly*)
Terrific. Sort of a shame he
couldn't ask me how I felt about
it, isn't it?

Brian moves to the closet, pulling off the windbreaker. Gale's expression has an edge of wariness to it, brought on by Piccolo's last remark. He sits up on the bed.

GALE

Look, if you want me out . . .

BRIAN

No, stay, I don't want you out.
I'm just steamed at the Old Man
for not putting me in the scrimmage
this afternoon.
　(*beat*)
Is that your wife?

GALE

Yeah.

BRIAN

She's pretty.

GALE

So's yours. And the little girl.

BRIAN

　(*still down*)
Thanks. I'm supposed to call her
tonight—tell her how I'm doing.
Be the shortest phone call in
history.

GALE

Maybe not.

When Piccolo looks over at him, Gale smiles.

GALE

Pic—they wouldn't assign us
to room together unless we *both*
made the team.

TIGHT ON BRIAN

He looks over at Gale and it hits him. From surly civility to beaming, whooping balls-out triumph. The angle widens as he moves to Gale, pulling him off the bed and shoving him toward the door.

>   BRIAN
> Come on! We've got to call our
> wives!

>   GALE
> I already called Linda, right
> after . . .

>   BRIAN
> That was just practice! This
> is for real! Come on!

And the two of them go tumbling out into the corridor.

INTERIOR—CORRIDOR—NIGHT— GALE AND BRIAN

They come barreling out of their room, laughing and giggling maniacally as they race toward us, then— stop. They're looking offstage warily, uneasily.

FULL SHOT—THE CORRIDOR

Atkins, O'Bradovich and Evey are standing a few feet away— Huge men, arms like hams, necks like tree stumps. Their expressions are insolent, challenging, though in no sense cruel. Each of them has an empty coffee can in hand—though not really empty. Each container holds a sticky-looking, evil-smelling con- glomeration of honey, cereal, sand, catsup, and whatever they could lay their hands on. They move in unison toward Brian and Gale.

ATKINS

Congratulations on making the team,
gentlemen. Well done.

EVEY

As you know, Coach Halas frowns on
the hazing of new men.

O'BRADOVICH

But now that you've made the team—
it's really like—you're one of
us.

All three have wooden spoons in the ooze, lifting the dripping, brown gunk for all to see. The two opposing forces, are motionless for a beat, then, in a second, they're all tearing down the hall. Gale and Brian are bent low, the three pursuers bellowing with the thrill of the hunt—howling savagely. The last words echo in the corridor as all the doors are opened and men stick their heads out to see which rookies are getting it now.

ATKINS

(*yelling*)
Welcome to the Chicago Bears!

DIRECT CUT TO:

NFL FOOTAGE OF SAYERS IN ACTION

Sayers returns a kickoff for a touchdown.

CUT TO:

INTERIOR—BEARS' LOCKER ROOM—DAY—
FULL SHOT

Gale is in front of his locker, just pulling off his jersey,
which is muddy and torn. Two reporters are on each
side of him. Piccolo, whose uniform looks as if he
stepped out of a catalog, is seated in front of his
locker, taking it all in with a certain objective humor.
Gale, typically, is ill at ease in this kind of situation.

REPORTER #1
Is playing in the NFL easier than
you thought it would be?

GALE
Only played one game. Not exactly
an expert.

REPORTER #2
But you didn't look as if you were
having too much trouble out there.

GALE
The blocks were there.

BRIAN
Sure is different from the way you
were talking last night, Gale.
    (*to reporters*)
He calls the offensive line the
"seven blocks of silly-putty."

GALE
Pic—

REPORTER #1

You're Brian Piccolo?

BRIAN

P–I–C–C–O–L–O, yes.

REPORTER #1

You two are the first black and
white to room together on the
team. Any problems so far?

BRIAN
(*straightfaced*)
Not as long as he doesn't use the
bathroom.

GALE

Pic—

DIRECT CUT TO:

NFL FOOTAGE

A long run from scrimmage by Sayers.

BRIAN (*Voice Over*)
Gale, when you run, do you think
about what you're doing, or do
you just do it?

GALE (*Voice Over*)
I just do it.

BRIAN (*Voice Over*)
Well, start thinking about it, will
you? I want to play, too.

DIRECT CUT TO:

INTERIOR—PIZZA PARLOR—NIGHT—
FULL SHOT

This is one of those pizza stands with a window out onto the street where passers-by can stop and indulge themselves—somehow feeling that when you buy pizza by the piece it's really not as bad as going in and ordering one. Grouped about one of the tables are Gale, Brian, and their wives, Joy Piccolo and Linda Sayers. They make a youthful and attractive quartet. They're at ease with one another, just now finishing off a casual, enjoyable evening on the town. The evening is typified by their present activity—listening to one of Brian's stories. He's telling it well, laughing as he does so, and it's a catching kind of thing for the girls. Gale, being Gale, allows himself a small smile, but little beyond that.

> BRIAN
> Now—picture this—Concannon
> calls a trap, see . . .
>   (*to Linda and Joy*)
> You know what a trap is?

> LINDA
>   (*unsure*)
> I think so, but—maybe . . .

> BRIAN
> Well—uh—all the linemen go one
> way and hopefully the defense
> guys go that way, too. If they do,

there's a big hole, see? If they
don't—bad news. Anyway—Concannon calls a trap up the middle,
Gale carrying the ball. It works
like they draw it on the blackboard.
Forty-three yards. Beautiful. So,
Halas sees Gale's winded; he tells
me to go in. So, I go in; Gale comes
out. We get in the huddle—Concannon decides he's going to get
foxy. He calls the *same* play. The
very same play. Last thing they'll
be looking for, he says. Now—the
trap play is also called the "sucker
play" because the defense really
looks bad when it works—and defenses
don't like to look bad—makes 'em
surly.

Joy, who's heard this story a hundred times already,
has started to laugh, anticipating Brian's big finish.

BRIAN

So—we come out of the huddle—
ball's snapped—all our linemen go
one way—and it's like I'm looking
at a team portrait of the Los Angeles
Rams—Hello, Deacon . . . Merlin, how's
the family . . . Rosey. . . .

Laughter from them all, ad-libs between the girls.
Gale's smile has broadened now and Brian's just having a fine old time.

BRIAN

I mean—I was afraid to get up.
I figured not everything was going
to come with me. . . .

JOY

(*nicely*)
You never saw anyone so black and
blue.

GALE

Yeah—it was like rooming with a
colored player again.

Gale grins—and the other three gape, looking at him
with expressions of shock. His smile turns uneasy,
bewildered. He glances at his fly, checks to make sure
there's no anchovy hanging off his chin.

LINDA

Gale—you told a *joke*.

BRIAN

Joy—did you hear it? The great
Stone Face from Kansas told a joke!

WIDE ANGLE

Brian turns to the other patrons, cupping his hands
about his mouth.

BRIAN

(*yelling*)
Chicago! There's hope for us
all! Sayers *speaks*!

GALE

Aw, come *on*, Pic . . .

But Gale's smiling, pleased with himself if the truth were known, as is Linda Sayers. The camera holds on them.

DIRECT CUT TO:

EXTERIOR—LOS ANGELES COLISEUM—
AERIAL VIEW (STOCK SHOT)

A football game is in progress, though the players are minute dolls from this altitude.

BRIAN (*Voice Over*)
Hey, Black Magic—listen to this
letter I got. "You must have been
raised with pigs to stay in the same
room with one of those darkies. You
must not have been taught anything
when you were a boy. You must have
crawled out from under some slimy rock."

GALE (*Voice Over*)
Is that all?

BRIAN (*Voice Over*)
Except for the usual: "Love, Mother."

NFL FOOTAGE OF A SAYERS RUN—
SLOW MOTION

This footage should be the most impressive of all, selling the power and grace of Sayers' ability.

BRIAN (*Voice Over*)
Magic—I think I'm going to write
you a speech.

GALE (*Voice Over*)
What kind of speech?

BRIAN (*Voice Over*)
Acceptance speech for "Rookie of the
Year." You can't miss.

GALE (*Voice Over*)
And I got to give a *speech?* You're
putting me on!

DIRECT CUT TO:

INTERIOR—BANQUET DAIS—NIGHT—
TIGHT SPOT

The air is filled with smoke, the offstage sound of a
speaker drones on. Most of the listeners we can see are
in their fifties, gray and full of cigar smoke and re-
spectability. Gale, Linda, Brian and Joy are on the dais
—the men in tuxedos, the women in formal gowns.
Brian has a crumpled piece of paper in his hand. He
leans into Gale, speaking in an urgent whisper.

BRIAN
From the top. One more time.

GALE
(*harried, by rote*)
I'd like to thank you all for this
honor, though it's really not right
to give it to one man. Football is
a—team sport, and I . . .

SPEAKER (*Offstage*)
Gale Sayers!

A spotlight floods the area and we hear offstage applause. Gale is urged to his feet by Brian and Linda. He moves toward the speaker's platform and microphone offstage.

TIGHT ON GALE

Petrified. All we can see is Gale; the harsh pinpoint of the carbon arc is centered on him with no residual spillage. He looks at the trophy for a second.

GALE

(*trembling*)
I'd—I'd like to thank you all
for this honor, though it's
really not right . . .

He stops. He stops because he can't think of the next word. It's gone. Nothing there. At this instant, staring out at all those eager faces, Gale Sayers has all the mental quickness and agility of a retarded newt.

ON BRIAN, JOY AND LINDA

The women agonize in the silence, trying to pray more words out of Gale. Brian can't believe it. He starts to slowly tear the speech up, shaking his head, grinning.

BACK ON GALE

A mouth like Death Valley. His lips move abortively.

GALE

Thank you.

ON BRIAN, JOY, LINDA

He tosses the pieces of paper in the air, like confetti, smiling fatalistically.

BRIAN

Who'd believe it—who'd ever
believe it . . .

DIRECT CUT TO:

EXTERIOR—SAYERS' HOUSE—NIGHT

BRIAN

Hey, Gale?

Gale holds on the porch. Linda waves a hand toward
the car, her words intended for Gale.

LINDA

Too cold out here. I'll warm your
side of the bed.

She moves into the house as Brian gets out of the car
and trots to Gale, both men with shoulders hunched
against the cold. Brian moves to him.

GALE

What do you want, man? It's freez-
ing out here!

BRIAN

Something I've got to tell you.

GALE

What is it?

Gale notes that there's an edge to Brian's voice, an
undercurrent of reluctance, shyness. Brian looks him
directly in the eye.

BRIAN

Joy and I had a long talk last
night—about whether or not I

should ask to be traded. We
decided that I wouldn't ask. I
like the guys on the team; I
like the town.
    (*beat*)
What I *don't* like is playing
second string.

GALE

    (*quietly*)
I don't blame you.

BRIAN

Now—*maybe* I've got a shot at
fullback. But I don't think
Halas thinks I'm big enough.
He'll probably go with Ralph Kunek.
The other spot is yours—and
that's the job I'm gunning for,
Gale.

Gale starts to reply, but Brian silences him with a
gesture.

BRIAN

Let me get it said.
    (*beat*)
I'm a better blocker than you are
and I'm as good a receiver. And
if I can't breakaway for sixty, I
can still get ten sixes, and it
adds up the same way. I'm going
to come into camp next year in the
best shape ever, and I think I've

got a realistic chance to blow you
out of the lineup. . . . And that's just
what I'm going to try to do.

GALE

I understand, man—that's your
job.

BRIAN

Yeah—but I don't like to do "a
job" on a friend.

GALE

(*small smile*)
Don't worry; you won't.

There's no anger between them, just resolve. After a
beat, there is a light tap on the car horn. Brian looks
at the trophy: he touches it lightly.

BRIAN

(*as Bogart*)
It's a Maltese Falcon, kid—get
this inside—and the free world
is safe.

With that, Brian moves back to the car, camera holding on Gale as he looks after his nutty friend, then
down to the trophy. He heads for the door.

DIRECT CUT TO:

INTERIOR—HALAS'S OFFICE—DAY—
ON PICTURE

Another team picture is being tacked on the wall, the
printing identifying it as last year's Bear aggregation.

DIRECT CUT TO:

EXTERIOR—PRACTICE FIELD AREA—DAY—
FULL SHOT

The team is lined up in two parallel rows, taking off
in the wind sprints in braces of two. Gibron stands
with Halas and McCaskey on the forty-yard line, snap-
ping the stopwatches on each pair.

GIBRON

(*calling*)
Caroline and Butkus up!

ANGLE TO LINE

J. C. Caroline and Dick Butkus take their places at the
goal line. They're dressed in T-shirts, shorts and football cleats. They crouch.

BUTKUS

A linebacker shouldn't have to
race a defensive back!

CAROLINE

You're not racing me; you're racing the clock.

BUTKUS

Still ought to get some kind of
handicap!

ANGLE TO PICCOLO

He is standing as the last man in one of the lines. Gale
can be seen approaching in the background.

BRIAN

You said the defensive backfield
was your handicap all last year,
Dick!

FULL SHOT

The "Go!" is shouted by Abe Gibron and the two
men take the other members of the team calling after
them. The next two men step up to the line.

ANGLE TO GALE AND BRIAN

Gale takes his position in the other line. Their look
to each other is friendly, but neither has precisely a
fix on what attitude is the working one. They speak as
the line moves forward. There are sounds of the other
men yelling offstage.

BRIAN

Hi. You just pull in?

GALE

Yeah. Would have been here this
morning, but the flight got fogged
in in Detroit. You look in good
shape.

BRIAN

I am. Worked hard this winter.
   (*beat*)
You talk to Linda today?

GALE

No. Why?

BRIAN

Thought she might have told you.
Joy's expecting again.

GALE

Really? That's great.

BRIAN

We think so.
(*beat*)
If—if it's a boy, we'd like to
name it after you.

Gale looks over at Brian, but the tone is a serious one, even a little bashful. They're next in line for the sprints.

GALE

No kidding?

GIBRON

(*yelling offstage*)
Sayers and Piccolo!

They both fall into starting positions.

BRIAN

Yeah—it's got a nice ring to it.
(*smiling*)
Spade Piccolo.

GIBRON

(*yelling offstage*)
Go!

FULL SHOT

Brian takes off, arms pumping, and Gale bursts into

helpless laughter, trying to run, but moving with the gait of a spastic on a rope bridge. Brian is past the forty at least three seconds before Gale, grinning from ear to ear.

ANGLE TO FORTY

Gale draws up from his leisurely sprint. They haven't even kept the clock on his effort.

> GALE
>
> Mind if I try it again?

> HALAS
>
> Might be a good idea.

Gale starts to retrace his steps to the goal line, then draws up, looking back to Gibron and Halas.

> GALE
>
> What was Pic's time like?

Gibron consults the clipboard.

> GIBRON
>
> Must be out to get you. . . . He's
> about half-a-second faster this
> year than last.

TIGHT ON GALE

He's not frightened, but properly impressed. He nods, taking it in. His expression denies his statement.

> GALE
>
> That's really terrific . . .

DIRECT CUT TO:

EXTERIOR—PRACTICE FIELD—DAY—
GALE AND BRIAN

They are both straining against the force of an Exer-Genie, perspiration popping from every pore, cheeks puffed out with effort. Gale quits first, but Brian keeps at it, face crimson as he pits himself against the device. Gale stands there, hands on hips, regarding his friend balefully. A deep breath, then Gale decides he's not going to be bested that easily and he starts in on the Exer-Genie with renewed dedication.

DIRECT CUT TO:

EXTERIOR—PRACTICE FIELD—DAY—
FULL SHOT

A number of men dot the area going through calisthenics. We find Gale and Brian doing sit-ups, each being helped by another player who anchors their feet. They're facing in opposite directions so that, as they come up, they're looking at each other. The looks are not hostile, but there's very little "give" in each man's expression.

DIRECT CUT TO:

EXTERIOR—PRACTICE FIELD—DAY—
FULL SHOT

The offense and defense are performing the one-on-one drill. This time, it's Brian who's the offensive back and the move he puts on the defensive man is a beauty. As Brian tears out of frame, we zoom in on Gale, impassive outwardly, but fully aware of what's going on.

DIRECT CUT TO:

INTERIOR—DORMITORY HALLWAY—NIGHT—FULL SHOT

Gale and Brian come in from the outside, both wearing light jackets, Brian carrying a large flat cardboard container, the shape telling us that his willpower has taken a hike once again.

> BRIAN
> That's why you'll never cut it, Sayers—pizza has magical properties that give Italian guys strength and speed.

> GALE
> Yeah—a lot of great Italian running backs, all right.

> BRIAN
> Yeah. Jim Brownanelli. Lennie Moorelli. All those guys.

ANGLE TO STAIRWAY

At the bottom is a bulletin board, where J. C. Caroline stands putting up a large sheet of paper. Brian moves by him, taking the stairs two at a time. Brian ad-libs a greeting, which is returned by J.C., who is too involved. Gale comes by.

> GALE
> What's that, J.C.?

CAROLINE
Starting lineups for the first
exhibition.

Gale's eye moves toward the landing of the second floor.

HIS POINT OF VIEW—ON WALL

The shadow of Brian Piccolo can be seen. His head turns slowly, listening.

BACK ON GALE AND CAROLINE

GALE
What's the backfield?

CAROLINE
(*as he goes*)
Concannon, Ralph Kunek, and you.

TIGHT ON GALE

If ever there were mixed emotions in a man, now is that time. He looks up.

HIS POINT OF VIEW—BRIAN'S SHADOW

Sagging, head lowered. A long beat, then Brian takes a breath, straightens his shoulders and moves off, the shadow disappearing.

BRIAN (*Offstage*)
Come on, Magic . . . pizza's getting
cold.

TIGHT ON GALE

He leans against the wall, disappointed and yet relieved at the same time. He looks toward the second-story landing once more, as we start to hear the growing roar of a large crowd, the unwavering roar of the hero seekers.

DIRECT CUT TO:

EXTERIOR—WRIGLEY FIELD—DAY—
NFL FOOTAGE

The stands are crowded with spectators. The day is damp and gray.

ANGLE TO FIELD—NFL FOOTAGE

The Bears are playing the 49ers with the ball.

ANGLE TO BEARS' BENCH—VARIOUS SHOTS

Gale's uniform, muddy and begrimed; Piccolo's not without a smudge or two. Halas and Gibron pace restlessly up and down the sidelines, yelling to the defensive unit, as are all the other players. Concannon is on the phones, listening intently.

ANGLE TO FIELD—NFL FOOTAGE

The ball is snapped to Brodie and he backpedals, looking for a receiver going deep.

ANGLE TO STANDS—LINDA AND JOY

Seated in the middle of the section for the wives of the players. All of them are relatively young and uncommonly attractive women. They're on their feet, yelling, urging the defensive unit to get to Brodie before he gets the pass off.

ANGLE TO FIELD—NFL FOOTAGE

Brodie gets the pass off, but it falls into the hands of a defensive back from the Chicago Bears.

ANGLE TO BENCH

Every man is on his feet yelling. There is a flurry of activity—Gale is pulling on his helmet, receiving a pat on the can from Brian. Concannon takes off the earphones and moves with the rest of the offensive team onto the field; all the action is under the all-seeing eye and far-reaching voice of Coach Halas.

ANGLE TO STANDS

The hubbub is only now trailing off. The women call down to their men.

LINDA

Go get 'em, Gale! You can do it, honey!

TIGHT ON JOY PICCOLO

Happy at this turn of events, but also painfully aware of something else, her eyes move from the field to the bench.

HER POINT OF VIEW—ON BRIAN

Back to the stands, helmet off, Number 41 paces restlessly back and forth along the sidelines. His attention is on the game, but the gaze drops a few times as inward moments take over.

ANGLE TO BEARS' HUDDLE

The circle is closed.

CONCANNON

Yours, Gale. Twenty-eight toss. South.
Lin. On three. *Break!*

FULL SHOT

The team comes out of the huddle, moving with precision into the chosen formation. Concannon looks over the defense, finds it within the tolerance of the play called and prepares to take the snap, calling out the signals in a rhythmic cadence.

DIFFERENT ANGLE

The ball is snapped and Concannon pivots, the move coordinated with the pulling of the guards and Gale's instantaneous break to his left. The ball is tossed spiraling back to Gale. He takes the pitch-out and has the ball well in hand as he starts to look for an opening in the upfield area.

ON LINDA AND JOY

Yelling. Cheering. Bouncing up and down with excitement.

ON BRIAN

He is at the water bucket, dipper poised as he steps to watch the play develop.

BACK ON GALE

Seemingly from nowhere, a San Francisco 49er uniform comes hurtling into frame and we freeze frame just before the shoulder of the player tears into Gale's knee. All crowd noises are killed. Only silence. The frame moves again now and we can see the awful impact. Freeze frame on this instant. The picture comes to life in short bursts as Gale crumples, the knee landing at an angle to set one's teeth on edge, in jerky, grainy images.

ON BRIAN

A freeze frame slowly moves forward half a step; he realizes what he's witnessing.

ON LINDA AND JOY

They are very much afraid of what they're seeing. Linda's hand flies to her mouth.

BACK ON GALE

He hits the ground, one hand already going to the knee, the ball forgotten about. He tries to get to his feet and the instant he puts any pressure on the knee, his head snaps back in reaction to the agony that assaults him. We freeze frame on Gale, every muscle contorted, and we hear the sound of a siren wailing, wailing, wailing.

HARD CUT TO:

EXTERIOR—SAYERS' HOME—DAY—FULL SHOT

The car, driven by Linda, pulls to a halt in the driveway. As she puts the gearshift into "Park," Gale opens the door on the passenger side and starts to get out. He's using two metal canes, the right leg swung out before him, stiff and unbending. His face is chiseled with tension and anger—cold, acid anger.

LINDA

Can I help?

GALE

No.

He makes his way slowly toward the front door, still not used to the canes, not yet using his body weight to help himself. Instead, it's a halting, unnatural motion—Painful to execute, more painful for Linda to watch. She hurries past him to open the front door.

INTERIOR—THE LIVING ROOM—DAY—
FULL SHOT

Gale comes in, no reaction to being home in his eyes. He moves to the first chair and sits. The look of the chair is not a "man's chair"; this would not be his normal place in the room. Linda comes in closing the door. She kneels by his side looking up at him hopefully.

LINDA

It's good to have you home, Gale.

GALE

Yeah. Good to be home.

But his eyes admit it was a reply made because it was the reply expected.

LINDA

Can I get you anything?

GALE

No. I'm fine.

LINDA

It's about lunch time. You want
a sandwich or anything?

GALE

Not hungry; you go ahead, though.

LINDA

Are you sure?

GALE

(*with an edge*)
Yes, I'm sure.

The emotional moat he's built up is too wide to be crossed at this point. Linda kisses him lightly on the cheek, then rises and moves to the kitchen. She pauses at the door looking back at him, a tentative smile on her face, but Gale's expression doesn't match or encourage the smile. Disheartened, Linda leaves the room.

TIGHT ON GALE

His hand moves to the injured knee, the cast large beneath the trouser leg. Alone, the mask falters slightly and the fear is unmistakable. Then, after a moment or two, we, and Gale, start to hear the sound of a man singing. And we've heard the song before—and the man. It's Brian singing the Wake Forest fight song. Gale looks with disbelief toward another door off of the living room. No mistaking. That's Piccolo, all right. Using the crutches, Gale pulls himself to an upright position and makes his way slowly across the room to the door. He pulls it open.

ANGLE DOWN BASEMENT STAIRWAY

The singing is louder now. A beat, then Brian's smiling face appears at the bottom. He's wearing old clothes, carries a crescent wrench in one hand.

BRIAN

Hey, Magic ... thought you'd never get here.

He moves back out of sight and we hear the sound of something metal being tapped upon. Gale enters frame and starts down the steps carefully.

GALE

Pic—what are you doing down there?

INTERIOR—BASEMENT—FULL SHOT—DAY

This is not a recreation room, but a place for storage and laundry, no ornamentation. The walls are cement block, gun-metal gray; the washer and dryer are in a corner. And opposite them, Brian Piccolo is tightening bolts on a metal framework that will eventually be used as a leg-lift machine. Gale negotiates the last few steps.

BRIAN

It's not a bad act, Gale, but Peg Leg Bates does it better.

GALE

(*indicating machine*)
What's that supposed to be?

BRIAN

It's not "supposed" to be any-

thing but what it is—a leg-
lift machine.

GALE

What for?

BRIAN

What *for?* Gale—getting that
knee back into shape is not
going to be a take-it-easy number. If you're afraid, that's
understandable, but . . .

GALE

(*hard*)
I am *not* afraid!

Piccolo is out of patience. He picks up the tools and
starts for the stairway.

BRIAN

(*quietly*)
You ought to be, Gale.

GALE

Pic, maybe you think this is a
real friendly thing you're doing,
but . . .

BRIAN

And you can put that in your
ditty bag, too, you stupid jack-
ass—friendship hasn't got
one thing to do with this . . .

Piccolo is halfway up the steps now. He stops, looking back at Gale, weighing whether or not to go on.

Sayers' expression is stubborn and angry, but no more so than Brian's. A beat, then Brian sits on one of the steps. The tension is still there, but under a tighter rein.

TIGHT ON BRIAN

He is a man trying to be honest about himself *to* himself.

> BRIAN
> Gale—when I was in high school—
> I was one of the best backs in
> the state. Unfortunately for me,
> *the* best back in the state, Tucker
> Fredrickson, went to the same
> school. And the colleges would
> come down to watch us and Tuck
> ended up at Auburn—and I ended
> up at Wake Forest. Good school,
> nice place, but not exactly center
> ring, you follow?
> (*beat*)
> So—I work my butt off at Forest.
> And my senior year—I led the nation
> in rushing and scoring . . .
> (*softly*)
> I mean—I led the *entire* nation.
> (*beat*)
> So, I look around for a pro team,
> and I pick the Bears. Then, who
> else comes to the Bears—Sayers.
> Big gun from a big school, and
> I'm number two all over again.

(*beat*)
Well, Gale—I'm number one guy
now, but for all the wrong reasons.
And if you don't come back one
hundred percent, people are always
going to say that I got in on a
pass, a lucky break, and I won't
take it that way.
   (*rises*)
I am going to beat you, Magic,
but it won't mean a thing unless
you're at your best, not one
second slower, one degree weaker.
I'm going to work your tail off
getting you into shape again—
for *my* sake.
   (*as he goes*)
I won't take the job from a cripple.

FULL SHOT

Brian turns and goes to the top of the stairs. He places
a hand on the knob, then looks back. Their eyes fence
for a moment, then Brian steps out. Gale stands there,
rage stilled, cooled, then turns, looking steadily at the
leg-lift machine. He moves to it, running his fingertips
over it lightly, seeking reassurance from the chilled
metal.

DIRECT CUT TO:

EXTERIOR—CITY PARK—DAY—ON GALE

It's a blustery, cold day. The wind drives ribbons of
dry snow along the walk. Gale moves towards us,

using a wooden cane, the limp noticeable, but not as bad as previously seen. He wears an overcoat, the collar turned up, and a grim expression. In his free hand he carries a small transistor radio. A sportscaster is heard over the sound of the wind.

> ANNOUNCER (*Voice Over*)
> And in Los Angeles, the Chicago
> Bears trimmed the Rams by a score
> of seventeen to sixteen. Quarter-
> back Jack Concannon was eight for
> fourteen passing, and the running
> game was ably manned by Brian
> Piccolo, who gained 105 yards in
> fourteen carries. Piccolo was
> awarded the game ball.

The Announcer is recounting times-out as Gale is adjacent to a litter basket. He stops for a beat, his back to us, then deposits the cane into the basket. His step seems to have more drive to it when he moves on.

DIRECT CUT TO:

EXTERIOR—PARK AREA—DAY—ON GALE

There's, if feasible, an early morning feel to the area as Gale, dressed in a sweatsuit, comes jogging toward us. His expression is stoic, the pace quite slow, the sort of speed one recommends to those just discharged from the hospital after hernial surgery. But, while slow, the pace is steady and dogged.

> DOCTOR FOX (*Voice Over*)
> (*filter*)
> Hello?

BRIAN (*Voice Over*)
(*filter*)
Doctor Fox? This is Brian Piccolo.
How's he doing?

DOCTOR FOX (*Voice Over*)
(*filter*)
Very well, I think. Though it's
boring going through those exercises all by yourself. It's
drudgery and it's painful, and a
lot of people just give up when
they're alone in that situation.

DIRECT CUT TO:

INTERIOR—SAYERS' BASEMENT—NIGHT—
TIGHT ON GALE

He is lying on his back, feet in the air, as he strains to
lift the platform bearing a sizable portion of weights.
He's drenched with sweat, puffing, coming to the
last repetition. We pan up from his face to the knee,
seeing the wicked-looking scar that creases the flesh.
As he starts to lift the platform, we pull back to reveal
Piccolo seated nearby, dressed in sports clothes. He
has a small kitchen egg timer in his hand. Gale lifts
the weights on the machine.

BRIAN
And—ten.
(*setting timer*)
Minute rest, then one more set.

GALE
Another one?

BRIAN

Last one tonight. Hang in there.

Gale remains on the floor under the weight machine. He sighs, getting his breath back.

BRIAN

How's the knee feel?

GALE

(*dispirited*)
Oh, one day it feels as strong as ever; the next day it's like I got spaghetti for ligaments.

BRIAN

(*beat*)
You know—if it doesn't come all the way back—it won't be the end of the world, Gale.

GALE

That so?

BRIAN

Football's terrific, man, but it's still just a job.

GALE

It's the only job I know how to do.
(*beat*)
I'm not like you—I can't talk and all that stuff.

BRIAN

Talking now . . .

GALE

It's different.

BRIAN

(*beat*)
You'll learn how to talk, once
you find something that's got to
be said.

The egg timer chirps once and Gale lifts his legs to the underside of the platform bearing the weights.

BRIAN

Third set. Ten reps. *Go.*

Gale starts to lift. The first three or four times go smoothly enough, but about halfway through the fifth one . . .

GALE

(*straining*)
I'll never make ten, man—no
juice left . . .

BRIAN

Don't bone me! Come on, Magic!
Hang tough! Five. Way to go—
six—lookin' good, Magic. Come
on . . .

GALE

No—way . . .

BRIAN

You aren't getting out that easy!
Come on! You can do it! Seven!

Fantastic! Three more, man!
Work on it! Are these the legs
of a murderer? Come on, Gale!
Eight! Got it! Two more!

GALE

No—way . . .

TIGHT ON BRIAN

He is leaning over Gale, mind seeking a ploy.

BRIAN

Can't make it, huh, nigger?
Nigger's giving up, is that it,
nigger? Is that what you're
doing, nigger?

TIGHT ON GALE

Looking up at Brian expressionlessly—then a stifled
laugh breaks from his lips. He smiles.

GALE

Come on, man—don't make me
laugh.

Gale starts to laugh and lets the weights come to rest
on the stops.

FULL SHOT

Gale starts to giggle and Brian just stands there without
any comprehension of how his maneuver could
have backfired so badly. Gale gets to his feet moving
about the basement, doing a real number on the befuddled
Piccolo.

GALE

(*melodramatic aside*)
I know what I'll do—I'll call
Gale a nigger and he'll do all
of them reps; he'll be so mad!
Too much! Nigger—nigger!

BRIAN

(*starting to laugh*)
Come on, man—lay off—I thought
I was being very clever. What
was I supposed to do—call you
a wop?

BRIAN

Now, *that'd* make me mad . . .

And they both start to laugh—silly, weary laughter. Absurd and nonsensical laughter. Contagious and childish and dumb. Impossible to explain and impossible, for the time being, to quell.

ANGLE TO TOP OF STAIRS

The door is opened by Linda and Joy. The laughter continues offstage. They exchange a baffled look.

LINDA

What's going on down there?

ANGLE DOWN STEPS

Gale and Brian appear still laughing foolishly. Gale takes a breath, getting himself under a short period of control.

GALE
You'll never believe it, babe.
Brian tried to call me a nigger!

And they both start to laugh again.

ANGLE TO LINDA AND JOY

They gaze down at their two loonies. It's one thing to suspect your husbands have gone bananas, quite another to see it so blatantly proven.

DIRECT CUT TO:

EXTERIOR WOODED AREA—DAY— LONG SHOT

Brian and Gale move along a narrow dirt road that winds through the trees. Their pace is no longer that of a jog, but one more suited to a brisk 880.

CLOSER—TRUCKING

We move back in front of the two of them as they run, both in control, arms pumping smoothly, the motion fluid and easy. After a few seconds, Brian looks over briefly at Gale, then he picks up the pace a little, opening a few yards between them. Gale takes this with some surprise, but matches Brian and closes the gap. But it's only temporary, for Brian ups the ante once more, the pace now at 440 clip. Gale's eyes flash as Brian moves away, but he picks it up again. He's shoulder to shoulder with Pic.

BRIAN
A beer for the first man to the
bridge!

GALE

You're on!

DIFFERENT ANGLE

Brian peels off from the road and crashes into the trees flanking the road. Gale is a little surprised at this cross-country route, but he's right after Brian, though he's got about five or six yards to make up due to the momentary hesitation.

ON BRIAN

There are no paths here, no easy routes. The trees and shrubs make it necessary to dart this way and that, hurdle logs, scramble up steep slopes and gullies. Brian is in the lead, but Gale's responding to the challenge, charging after him at full bore.

VARIOUS CUTS—THE CHASE

The two of them are bound together by an invisible rope, though the rope has developed a tendency to shrink slightly. It's almost imperceptible, but Gale is making up ground on Brian. They come to a creek bed five or six inches deep, and as they go splashing through it, we go to slow motion—droplets exploding into the sunlight, the two men calling on reserves from deep within, approaching that point inside themselves that's way beyond pain, on the far side of agony. The small stream dwindles to loose shale.

THE FALL

A scant step behind Piccolo, Gale loses his footing on the stones and takes a head-over-heels tumble, a really bad one, pinwheeling over and over violently. Piccolo halts immediately, looking back at Gale with concern.

ON BRIAN

He is gasping for breath, looking to Gale.

ON GALE

He meets Brian's look. Every breath hurts, sears. He glances down at the knee, then stands slowly, brushing the stones from the palms of his hands. He meets Brian's look. He nods.

FULL SHOT

Like catapults, they both turn and take off.

THE MEADOW—TRUCKING

They burst out of the trees, Gale a step behind. This is the final all-out sprint for the tape. Nothing held in reserve at this point, they pull great gulps of air in, straining, eyes frozen on the finish up ahead. And with each step, Gale moves up. An inch, no more, but that inch is repeated with each step, every stride bringing him closer to Brian's shoulder.

LONG SHOT

As they near a small wooden footbridge, moving, it seems, as one, mirror images of black and white.

ANGLE TO THE BRIDGE

They both literally hurl themselves at the imaginary tape and go tumbling across the bridge with their momentum, sprawling in the soft grass on the other side.

ANGLE ACROSS BRIDGE

They are both lying there, having given it all they had
to give. They're shiny as seals with perspiration, their
eyes bright with fatigue, focusing on the blue sky
overhead. After a long moment, they both sit up,
shaky smiles on their faces, though they're still puffing like a Saint Bernard in Palm Springs.

BRIAN

I—think—I—owe—you—a—
beer.

GALE

(*shakes head*)
I—think—I—owe—you—a—
lot—more—than—that.

BRIAN

Yeah—you're—healthy.

GALE

Yeah.

And they look at each other, the expressions of both
growing a little serious, aware that, as friends, they
are still competitors; there's only one brass ring on
this merry-go-round.

GIBRON (*Voice Over*)
What do you think training camp
is? You think training camp is
some kind of picnic? Is that
what you think? Because there's
no man assured of a job around

here, let me tell you, and if you
think you are, then you got one
more think comin', gentlemen!

As Gibron's voice started to come over, we also started
to hear the sounds of the Chicago Bears calling out a
cadence as they go through their calisthenics.

HARD CUT TO:

EXTERIOR—PRACTICE FIELD—DAY—
LONG SHOT

The team is facing J. C. Caroline, who is leading them
in a series of side-straddle hops, the chorus of yells
loud and vibrant.

CUT TO:

EXTERIOR—PRACTICE AREA—DAY—
FULL SHOT

The backs step through the ropes, knees high. We
pick up Gale going through the obstacle course, with
Brian right behind him, both handling it with relative
ease. We pan them, then all of them leave the frame
to hold on the grizzled features of Coach Halas. His
eyes are masked by dark glasses, but there's a smile
tugging on the corners of his mouth.

DIRECT CUT TO:

INTERIOR—DORMITORY ROOM—NIGHT—
ON GALE

The playbook is in front of him. We pan across the
room to find Brian, same look, same activity. A beat,

then there is a knock on the door. Brian moves to answer it.

FULL SHOT

Brian opens the door and reacts with some surprise on seeing Coach Halas standing in the hallway. He nods pleasantly. Gale, too, is surprised and sits up.

> HALAS
>
> Hello, Brian. Mind if I come in
> for a moment?

> BRIAN
>
> No, no. Of course not. Come on
> in, Coach.

And Halas comes in, moving by Brian. The two young men look to each other, neither having any notion that might explain this unprecedented visit.

> HALAS
>
> How's the knee, Gale?

> GALE
>
> Fine, Coach. Feels strong.

> BRIAN
>
> Look, if you want to talk to Gale,
> I can just walk on down to . . .

> HALAS
>
> No, actually, I'd like to talk to
> both of you.

Chilling portent. They both smile, as does Halas, but

only the Old Man's has any relaxation in it. Long beat.
Thoat clearings from Gale and Brian.

BRIAN
Well—uh—how do things look
this year, Coach?

HALAS
Fine. Just fine. Matter of fact,
there's one boy I'm very impressed
with. Brian, I wouldn't be surprised to see him replace you as
number two halfback.

Halas lets the moment run on for a second.

HALAS
Because I'm making you number one
fullback.

TIGHT ON BRIAN

He sits there looking at Halas much as Papa Dionne
must have looked at the doctor.

ON GALE

Beaming, really and deeply pleased for his friend.

GALE
Hey, Pic—you and me the starting backfield—what do you say?

FULL SHOT

Brian just shakes his head back and forth, an empty
smile flopping about on his face.

GALE

Coach—I didn't think it was
possible—but I think you
finally found a way to shut him
up!

HARD CUT TO:

NFL FOOTAGE—ALTERNATING BETWEEN
RUNS OF PICCOLO AND SAYERS

GALE (*Voice Over*)

Hey, Pic?

BRIAN (*Voice Over*)

Yeah?

GALE (*Voice Over*)

You know you got a four point three
rushing average?

BRIAN (*Voice Over*)

No, man, but hum a few bars and
I'll see if I can fake it.

GALE (*Voice Over; Overlapping*)
Awe, *Pic* . . .

The last NFL cut is designed to intercut with:

EXTERIOR—ANGLE TO FOOTBALL FIELD—
END ZONE

Brian breaks through a hole in the center of the line,
keeping his feet as he gets to the end zone, flipping
the ball high into the air. The first person to him is
Gale, slapping him exuberantly on the back as they
move with their teammates toward the bench.

DIRECT CUT TO:

INTERIOR—LOCKER ROOM—DAY—
FULL SHOT

The team is being weighed in, Gibron by the scales, sliding the weights up and down the bar and calling out the result for each man. There is some good-natured catcalling as some of the larger linemen are weighed in and most of it is coming from Brian, who is next in line with Gale close behind him.

CLOSER ANGLE

The lineman moves off the scale and Brian takes his place. Gibron starts to readjust the weights for Brian.

BRIAN

Scrimmage tomorrow, Abe. Going
to give us any trick plays?

GIBRON

Only trick I'd like to give you
is how to keep some meat on you.
You're down another pound.

BRIAN

But what's there is choice; admit
it.

GIBRON

Two-o-six and a quarter. Skin-
niest fullback in the league.

BRIAN

Gibron, you run the fat off us,
then complain that we're too thin.
You're a hard man to please.

Brian grins, used to Gibron's grumbles, and moves off. Gale is next in line.

> **GIBRON**
>
> Ought to tell your Italian friend
> to load up on the pasta.

> **GALE**
>
> Probably just wants to be quicker,
> Gibron.

> **GIBRON**
>
> Well, it ain't workin'. He lost
> ten pounds and he's half a second
> slower over a forty-yard sprint.
> Lighter *and* slower don't total
> out to much of a threat, you know.
>   (*checks the weight*)
> One ninety-nine. Next.

We move with Gale as he steps off the scale, camera closing on him. He glances off at Gibron, then in the direction taken by Brian. His eyes are puzzled; it's a weird combination Gibron has pointed out. Strange. Unsettling. Gale lets it sink in.

DIRECT CUT TO:

NFL FOOTAGE OF GALE AND BRIAN

Running the ball, alternating. Two cuts, the first being the best footage of Piccolo as either runner or receiver, the last being a punt return by Sayers that goes all the way. This final cut, the punt return, is to lead directly into the following staged sequence.

ANGLE TO BEARS' SIDELINE

Gale comes off the field with the rest of the punt-return unit, among whom is Brian. Typically, Gale barely smiles at the congratulations he gets. He moves to the bench and sits, Brian by his side. They pull off their helmets, eyes on the action of the game.

CLOSER ANGLE—GALE AND BRIAN

Both winded, but with one difference. Gale is clearly buoyed up, exhilarated. Brian simply seems tired.

GALE

Nice block.

BRIAN

Thanks.
 (*beat*)
Must be ninety million pounds
of pollen in the air.

They look toward the end zone as a cheer tells us the extra point is good. We can hear Gibron calling for the kickoff unit to take the field. Gale glances over at Brian casually and might see what we are now noting. Gale's respiration is swiftly slowing down, approaching normal. Brian's is not, he's still winded and badly so. Brian rises, moving for the water bucket near the phone desk. Gale watches him, then rises, moving for the sidelines to view the upcoming kickoff, camera moving with him. He finds an opening in the men standing there, then, in the hush just prior to the kicker's runup—the sound of Brian coughing. Gale turns back.

HIS POINT OF VIEW—ON BRIAN

The roar of the crowd overwhelms the sound of Piccolo's coughing. He takes down a fair amount of water, but that doesn't help. The angle widens to include Gale as Brian joins those on the sidelines. There are a number of men filing by them as the kickoff unit and defensive team change places. Brian coughs once more, though it's more evident in the motion of his shoulders and chest than in a sound; he's making an effort to stifle the cough.

GALE

You ought to get Fox to give you
something for that hay fever.

BRIAN

He did. Doesn't help. The only
thing I'm allergic to is Ray
Nietschke.
   (*yelling*)
All right, Butkus! Stick it in
their ear, babe!

Brian moves off, back toward the bench. Gale looks to the playing field, but his thoughts are elsewhere. He glances back.

HIS POINT OF VIEW—ANGLE TO PICCOLO

Seated once more on the bench, his helmet off, still using more effort than one would expect to get his wind back. He sees Gale looking at him and smiles, giving a "thumbs-up" sign.

ON GALE

Nodding, returning both the smile and the sign, and both are, at one and the same time, lies and prayers.

DIRECT CUT TO:

INTERIOR—BEARS' LOCKER ROOM—DAY—
FULL SHOT

Most of the players are dressed now, or seated in front of their lockers tying their shoes. We find Halas as he comes out of his office, his expression somber. He nods goodbye to some of the players heading out of the locker room, then moves for a door off of the main area.

INTERIOR—WHIRLPOOL ROOM—DAY—
FULL SHOT

Gale is in the whirlpool, head back, eyes closed, letting the swirling water take away some of the residual aches and pains of this afternoon's combat. Halas comes into the room and closes the door, the sound of the door drawing Gale's attention. Halas pulls up a stool and sits, drained, enervated.

GALE

Lookin' at you, I'd never know
we won the game.

HALAS

(*small smile*)
I don't feel very much like a
winner at the moment.

GALE

Why not?

A deep breath, a gathering of his forces.

HALAS

Gale, I'm sending Brian Piccolo
back to Chicago. He won't make
the rest of the road trip with
us. Ralph Kunek's going to start
next week.

GALE

(*beat*)
Why?

HALAS

Because I've had a policy on this
team from the very start—the
best player plays, no exceptions.
And right now—Kunek is the best
player.

GALE

Look, a lot of guys take a while
to get on track for a season, slow
starters, and . . .

HALAS

(*finishing for him*)
And Brian Picccolo has never been
one of those guys, Gale. He's
always been in shape, able to give
one hundred percent. But he isn't doing that
anymore, and that worries me.
(*with regret*)
I don't know why—something physi-

cal—or whether he's got personal
problems, something with his wife
or children—but the truth is that
something is taking the edge off
of him—and I want to find out
what that something is. For his
sake and the team's. Can't afford
to lose a back that good.

GALE

(*resigned*)
When's he going to find out?

HALAS

Abe's telling him now. That's
why I didn't want you to go right
back to the hotel.

GALE

Wouldn't want to be in Abe's shoes
about now . . .

HALAS

I wouldn't want to be in *your*
shoes about ten minutes from now.

And as Gale contemplates the buzz saw he's likely to
walk into.

DIRECT CUT TO:

INTERIOR—HOTEL ROOM—NIGHT—
ON SUITCASE

A bundle of wadded-up clothes is thrown into the
suitcase. We pull back to reveal Piccolo in the act of
packing, moving from closet and dresser to the suit-

case on the bed. Gale maintains a low profile, not wanting to draw any fire from Brian, who would swing at the Flying Nun right about now.

BRIAN

Who'd believe it? I mean, really, who'd believe it!

GALE

Halas just wants you to see the doctor, and . . .

BRIAN

Halas doesn't know what he wants! Gibron's his boy and you should have heard *that* lecture! Kept telling me to patch things up with Joy. I tell him things are fine with me and Joy. And he just smiles that Father Flanagan smile of his and says I shouldn't be afraid to level with him. Dear Abby in a jockstrap!

GALE

Pic, be fair, now. Doctor Fox says that . . .

BRIAN

Oh, spare me any crud about our great team doctor. Wants me to get a physical for the cough, right? No allergy. Then what is it, I say! Want to hear what

he says? *Could* be a virus. *Could*
be a staph infection. *Could* be
any one of a thousand things.
It's like being treated in a Chi-
nese restaurant—two from column
A, three from column B!

GALE

He's just trying to help, Pic . . .

A beat, then Brian sits on the bed, calming somewhat,
but still angry and frustrated.

BRIAN

Yeah—I suppose you're right—
but it's all so pointless, Gale.
Hell, I know perfectly well what's
wrong with me.

TIGHT ON BRIAN

He looks over at Gale, eyes radiating sincerity.

BRIAN

Gale—I think I'm pregnant.

DIRECT CUT TO:

EXTERIOR—BALTIMORE MEMORIAL STADIUM
—DAY—ESTABLISHING STOCK SHOT

The fans are threading their way into the stadium,
pennants and air horns in evidence.

INTERIOR—VISITING TEAM LOCKER ROOM—
DAY—FULL SHOT

The Chicago Bears suit up. Linemen pound each
other's shoulder pads to a tighter fit. Some of the players

sit in front of their lockers, wide-eyed, seeing nothing, nearly catatonic. Others move about nervously, bouncing on the balls of their feet, trembling with caged energy.

ANGLE TO TRAINING TABLE

Gale gets his ankle wrapped tightly with adhesive tape. His face has the look of a carving, somber, dark, guarded. The trainer finishes the job and Gale nods his thanks, moving off the table, another man following behind him at once. We move with him as he strides toward a door at the other end of the locker room. He passes by Gibron who is going over the attack plan with Concannon and the second-string quarterback, past linemen who are simply yelling at each other, wordless growls and bellows. Gale stops in front of the door bearing the word: Coach. He knocks on the door.

HALAS (*Offstage*)

Come in.

INTERIOR—THE COACH'S OFFICE—DAY—
FULL SHOT

Halas is seated behind the desk, hat and dark glasses on. Ed McCaskey is at a water cooler in the corner, drawing a paper cup out of the container, using the water to wash down a pill. At first, both men seem quite normal, but it's a façade and one that's being eroded with each passing second.

GALE

Which end of the field you want me
to take if we lose the toss?

McCaskey and Halas stare at him for a second, then look to each other. Gale is a little baffled by the delay; the question is a standard one. Some kind of communication is going on between the two older men. They nod.

HALAS
Come on in, Gale. Close the door.

There is something in that tone, something vulnerable and sad, out of key. Gale steps into the room and closes the door as requested. There is a short silence, each of the other men hoping they'll not have to take the lead.

HALAS
Gale—we've just had a phone
call from Memorial Hospital . . .

Halas removes the glasses. His eyes are red. He takes a breath.

HALAS
Brian Piccolo has cancer.

RIGHT ON GALE

Awe has within it an element of fear, of facing something so basic, so large, that one cannot ever truly cope with it. Gale reacts with prayerful disbelief and awe.

GALE
Oh, God . . .

FULL SHOT

Halas kneads the bridge of his nose, the eyes closed

as if hoping the curtain of his eyelids will allow time
for a scene change.

HALAS
They've scheduled an operation
for tomorrow morning.

GALE
(*feeling*)
An operation to do what?

MC CASKEY
(*evenly, calmly*)
Gale, they've got to remove part
of Brian's right lung.

TIGHT ON GALE

This strikes him like a scrotal whiplash. He starts to
sink weakly into a nearby chair, and as he does so the
frame freezes several times, giving the same look asso-
ciated with the knee injury. As he sinks into the chair,
the image moves with stuttering, uneven speed.

HALAS (*Offstage*)
The doctors don't have any explanation,
Gale. It must be something Brian has
carried around inside him all his life.
What set it off, they don't know. As
to whether or not they found it in time
—well, they don't know that either,
I'm afraid.

FULL SHOT

Gale's eyes are glazed. His spirit has been blindsided.
Halas and McCaskey are no less affected; they've

merely had a few moments more to apply an emotional poultice.

> MC CASKEY
> *(to Halas)*
> Who tells them?

ANOTHER ANGLE

Halas sighs, nodding with reluctant acceptance.

> HALAS
> I know. It's my responsibility
> and I'll ...

> GALE
> *(interrupting)*
> I'll tell them.

> HALAS
> *(surprised)*
> You, Gale?

> GALE
> *(rising)*
> That's right, me. I'll tell them.
> Let's go.
> *(to McCaskey)*
> Does Linda know?

> MC CASKEY
> I don't think so ...

> GALE
> Call her and tell her.

He pulls open the door, looking to Halas. The Coach and McCaskey trade a swift look, then Halas gets to his feet. As he moves to the door, McCaskey picks up the phone on the desk and starts to dial.

INTERIOR—THE LOCKER ROOM—DAY—FULL SHOT

Halas and Gale come out of the Coach's room. Halas's presence is noted quickly and the players gather around in a loose semicircle, all the pregame rituals at an end. Gale appears very much in control of himself, in command of the situation. After a great injury, it takes a while before the pain is *really* felt. That "while" is passing.

> **HALAS**
> (*to players*)
> Gale has got something he'd like
> to say to you all. Gale . . .

TIGHT ON GALE

He attempts to sustain eye contact with the other members of the team, but it swiftly becomes clear to him that he can't make it. Initially, his voice is strong and clear, but he can't hold it there for long.

> **GALE**
> You—you all know that we hand
> out a game ball to the outstanding
> player. Well, I'd like to change
> that a little. We just got word
> that Brian Piccolo—that he's
> sick. Very sick. It looks like
> —uh—that he might not ever

play football again—or—for
a long time . . .
(*beat*)
And—I think we should all dedicate
ourselves to—give our maximum
effort to win this ball game, and
give the game ball to Pic. We
can all sign it and take it up to
him at the hosp . . .

His voice tightens with abrupt anguish. He turns away, hiding his tears.

GALE
(*continuing, softly*)
Oh, my *God* . . .

FADE OUT:

FADE IN:

EXTERIOR—HOSPITAL—DAY—
ESTABLISHING SHOT—(STOCK)

Hold a beat.

DIRECT CUT TO:

INTERIOR—BRIAN'S HOSPITAL ROOM—
DAY—TIGHT ON BRIAN

Garbed in hospital gown, looking strangely out of place, a young man of two hundred pounds is in something approximating a doll's wardrobe. He's grinning from ear to ear, holding up the front page of the sports section, the headline of which reads: COLTS DUMP BEARS 24-21.

BRIAN (*Voice Over*)
Fantastic! Who'd believe it!
Sayers, you've got great moves on
the field, but in the locker room,
I've got to tell you, you're a klutz!

It is important here to stress that the humor is *not* role playing; the fun has no element of stiff upper lip in it. Bittersweet is for chocolate, not for Brian Piccolo.

BRIAN
When you dedicate a game to someone,
you are then supposed to go
out and *win* the game, idiot! Pat
O'Brien never said, "Blow one for
the Gipper," you know.

FULL SHOT

Revealing the "sickroom," a misnomer if ever there was one. Gale and Jack Concannon stand at the end of the bed. At a small table near the window, the flowers and cards have been cleared away by J. C. Caroline and a few other players. In place of these niceties, they are opening up two cartons of pizza and two six-packs of beer. Joy Piccolo stands next to her husband, looking at the food being laid out with hapless affection and bewilderment.

GALE
Bad—you are so bad.

CAROLINE
We probably would have won if
Concannon had called that trap

play more, but he hates to use
it unless you're there for the
repeat.

The men at the table have started putting pieces of
pizza on paper napkins and begin to distribute same.

JOY
Brian, do you think this is such
a good idea? I mean, pepperoni
pizza and beer *isn't* on your diet.

BRIAN
Joy—are you telling me as I
lie on this bed of pain, my body
whittled away at by a ruthless
band of strangers with Exacto
knives—are you telling me I
can't have any *pizza?*

Joy studies Brian, then looks to the other men, each
with a can of beer and a slice of pizza in hand. She
shakes her head, exasperated and loving them all very
much.

JOY
Pass the pizza, please . . .

With smiles, the others crowd around the bed as Joy
moves to the table to obtain a beer for herself and
Brian. After a second or two to get the first bite down.

BRIAN
Hey—who wants to see my scar?

Instant negative replies from them all. As these trail

off, the door is opened offstage and they all look around.

DIFFERENT ANGLE—ON NURSE

She gazes at her patient, who has just had a lung removed, as he visits with his wife and friends, all of whom have a piece of pizza and a can of beer in hand. Doctor Welby never mentioned this to her.

NURSE

Out! Now! No discussion! *Out!*

FULL SHOT

Gale, Butkus, Concannon, Caroline and Mayes quickly gather up the pizza cartons and six-packs of beer and head for the door, ad-libbing farewells, ducking their heads like schoolboys as they pass by the nurse. Gale is the last in line. Joy straightens up from kissing Brian goodbye.

BRIAN

Hey, take Gale down and have him
give that little girl his autograph,
will you?
(*to Gale*)
Little girl I met the day I came
in here. We had our operations on
the same day. Told her I'd get your
autograph. You don't mind, do you?

GALE

No problem. Be glad to.

JOY

I'll see you tonight.

He blows a kiss at her and they all leave. The nurse holds for a second in the door, reinforcing her disapproval of Brian's ways. She sighs and steps out of the door. Once it's closed, Brian throws back the covers and puts his feet over the side. There's a good deal of strain and discomfort involved, but it's well within Brian's tolerance. He stands with his back to the window, then starts for the door, his gait a shuffle.

BRIAN

There he goes, sports fans—can
you believe it—power, speed,
grace, and agility all wrapped
up in . . .

Brian halts as the door is opened once again by the nurse. Their eyes fight to a draw.

BRIAN

Don't come any closer, Miss Furman.
White lisle stockings turn me on!

DIRECT CUT TO:

CHILDREN'S WARD—ANGLE TO NURSES' STATION

The walls here are festooned with crayon drawings made by the patients. The nurses' station has a number of stuffed animals on the counter. As Joy and Gale approach, one of the nurses hangs up the phone and turns to them with a pleasant smile.

NURSE #2

May I help you?

JOY

My name's Mrs. Piccolo. My
husband's a patient on the third
floor and he told me about a
little girl—Patti Lucas—
who wanted this gentleman's
autograph.

The Nurse nods nicely, holding up a finger as she flips
swiftly through the Rolodex in front of her.

NURSE #2

I'm sorry, Mrs. Piccolo—Patti
isn't with us anymore.

JOY

Well, do you have a home address?
My husband wanted her to have the
autograph very much.

NURSE #2

(*beat*)
Mrs. Piccolo—Patti's dead. She
passed away early this morning.

Gale places his hand gently on Joy's shoulder. Both
of them react inwardly to the Nurse's words. Joy nods,
forcing a smile mouthing the "thank you," though her
voice is absent. Gale is a few feet behind her as they
start back for the elevator bank.

DIRECT CUT TO:

NFL FOOTAGE OF GALE IN AN END RUN,
PREFERABLY SLOW MOTION

The crowd noise is at a frenzied peak, then the frame
freezes.

BRIAN (*Voice Over*)
Look at that knee, will you? That
thing is really beautiful!

EXTERIOR—HOSPITAL GROUNDS—DAY—
FULL SHOT

Brian is wheeled out into a shaded area of the hospital lawn. He's looking at a sports magazine which he
holds up so Joy can see the picture. They stop beneath
a large tree bordering the walk.

BRIAN
Nothing wrong with that knee; I'll
tell you that.

JOY
Congratulations, Doctor Piccolo.

BRIAN
Yeah—but you know what—I've
been thinking. With Gale healthy,
and Ralph Kunek healthy—I'm
going to have a rough time getting
back into the lineup next year.
And I was thinking—what's so
difficult about being a kicker? I
mean, I wonder if it's something
you can teach yourself. 'Cause you
don't need a lot of wind or stamina
or size . . .

He looks down at Joy and the look on her face is
weakening, hopeful still, but with more effort required

on her part with each day that goes by. Brian reads
that look like a compass.

BRIAN

All right, Gloomy Gus—what do
you think of my brainstorm?

JOY

(*floundering*)
Well—I don't know, Brian—I'm
no expert on kickers and things . . .

BRIAN

You just did an end run that Red
Grange would be proud to call his
own.

JOY

Don't make fun of me, Brian. I'm
scared.

BRIAN

(*evenly*)
What of?

JOY

(*sputtering with disbelief*)
What *of*? What *of*? You can't be
serious! You know perfectly well
what of!

BRIAN

(*absolutely sincere*)
No, I don't, Joy. I swear to
God I don't.

(*taking her hands*)
Look—I'm no idiot.—This thing
is bad—I know that—but it's
a detour, Joy—that's all. It's
not going to stop me because I'm
not going to *let* it stop me. No
way . . .
(*quietly*)
I've got too much to do yet, Joy.

DIFFERENT ANGLE

Her face in his hands, Brian bends to kiss Joy. As
their lips meet, we start to boom up and back. Joy
leans her head against Brian's knee, his hand stroking
her hair.

DIRECT CUT TO:

NFL FOOTAGE OF SAYERS

Fielding a punt, signaling for a fair catch, then decid-
ing to let it roll. And roll it does, further and further
back toward his own goal. By the time he realizes he
should have caught it, there are a number of defensive
men all around the ball, making any return impossible. From the time the ball struck earth and took off,
we have heard *OVER THIS:*

BRIAN (*Voice Over*)
Pick it up! Pick it up, dummy!
Gale! Joy, look at him!

NURSE (*Voice Over*)
Now, Mister Piccolo, calm down.

BRIAN (*Voice Over*)
Calm down? How can I calm down?
You'd think the ball was wearing
a white sheet.

DIRECT CUT TO:

INTERIOR—HOTEL ROOM—NIGHT—FULL
SHOT

Gale is on the bed, shoes off, talking on the phone
with Brian, the mood one of good-natured give-and-
take. Seated on the other bed is a football player,
Gale's new roommate. There is a room-service cart in
evidence, remnants there of sandwiches and glasses
of milk. We intercut this with Brian in his hospital
room. There is no one else present with Brian.

GALE
Well, I was going to catch it,
but when it started coming down,
I said I wonder what Pic would
do in a situation like this, and
ducking seemed to be the answer.

BRIAN
Well, at least you won the game.

GALE
That's right.

BRIAN
Didn't dedicate this one to me,
though, did you?

In the hotel room, there is a knock on the door. The
player goes to answer it. He opens the door to reveal

a hotel official, who exchanges a few words with the football player, then is allowed into the room.

GALE

Nope. Dedicated this one to Butkus.

BRIAN

Why?

GALE

He threatened us.
(*beat*)
How you doin'? Pic? Really?

BRIAN

Hanging in there, Magic. Doing what they tell me to do. You could do me a favor, though.

GALE

You got it. Name it.

BRIAN

Call Joy, will you? When she left tonight, she was really down. I never saw her that down.

GALE

I'll call her as soon as I get back.

BRIAN

Thanks, I appreciate it.

GALE

Okay. Goodnight.

BRIAN

Goodnight.

Gale hangs up, then looks a question to the hotel clerk, whose presence he has registered while talking to Brian.

HOTEL OFFICIAL

Mister Sayers, while you were on
the phone, there was a lady who
called. She seemed very upset.

He hands Gale a piece of folded paper. Gale unfolds it.

HOTEL OFFICIAL

I hope I've not overstepped my
authority.

PLAYER

I'm sure you did the right thing.
Thank you very much.

He ushers the hotel official out the door, closes it, then glances back at Gale. The young black man sags, drained.

GALE

It's Joy Piccolo. She says it's
urgent.

DIRECT CUT TO:

INTERIOR—PICCOLO LIVING ROOM—NIGHT—ON CLOCK

The time is 3:30. We pull back to reveal Joy, in robe

and slippers, pouring coffee for Gale and Linda. The Sayers have dumped their coats on the couch.

                    JOY
        I know it's an awful thing, to
        make you fly all the way back
        here in the middle of the night,
        but . . .

                    GALE
        It doesn't bother me, so don't
        let it bother you.

Joy smiles feebly and sits, her hands tightly intertwined, struggling to maintain her composure. A long beat.

                    LINDA
        Just say it, Joy . . .

Joy nods, a small childlike move.

                    JOY
        They found more of the tumor . . .

The tears come. Her face twists, crumpling under the terror and the fear. Linda moves to her, holding her, both women rocking back and forth. Linda offering presence and mute compassion but knowing better than to voice any bromides. Gale swallows bitterly, probably wishing he was strong enough to cry. He pulls a handkerchief out of his pocket and places it on the coffee table within Joy's reach. She nods her appreciation, dabbing at her eyes, pulling in the air with calming effect.

JOY

They told me today—they want to
operate again—and I was going to
tell Brian—but—I couldn't, Gale.
I don't know whether or not he can
take the disappointment. And if he
can't—I know *I* can't.
　(*beat*)
The doctor is going to tell him
tomorrow morning. If you could be
there when he finds out—it might
help.

TIGHT ON GALE

Some few times when evasion is a luxury that cannot
be allowed, some tasks must be carried out, some
pains endured because another's pain is the greater.

GALE

I'll be there, Joy.

DIRECT CUT TO:

INTERIOR BRIAN'S ROOM—DAY—ON
FOOTBALL GAME

This is a "board game" with charts and dice and
miniature scoreboard, much along the lines of the
Sports Illustrated game. As we pull back, we find
Brian and Gale seated on opposite sides of the small
table near the window. They both roll their respective
dice.

GALE

What'd you try?

BRIAN

End run.

GALE

Oh, Lordy—I was in a blitz.

Brian starts to consult the complicated chart that will give him the results of the play.

GALE
(*indicating game chart*)
Well—did you gain or what?

DIFFERENT ANGLE

The door is opened by Mr. Eberle, a nervous, uncertain sort, more at home with facts and figures than flesh and blood. He's dressed in slacks, lab coat and bow tie. A name tag hangs from the lapel of the lab coat. Brian looks up with a smile.

BRIAN

Hi. Can I help you?

EBERLE

Well, I'm sorry if I'm disturbing
anything . . .

BRIAN

Don't worry—I can beat him
later. What can I do for you?

EBERLE
(*rummaging through papers*)
I know this as a bother at a time
like this, Mr. Piccolo, but
hospitals have their rules and

regulations, you see, and I'll
need your signature on this
surgical consent for the operation.

He hands Brian the piece of paper, but Brian is scarcely aware of it. He looks at Eberle uncomprehendingly, stunned. Gale is searching for a way to ease this, but before he can locate his voice, Eberle notes the bewilderment on Brian's face.

EBERLE

The doctor *has* been here, hasn't he?
He's talked with you, I mean?

BRIAN

No . . .

EBERLE

(*looking to watch*)
Oh—well, I suppose I might be
running a little ahead of my schedule
today. Perhaps I better come back
after the doctor has . . .

BRIAN

What would the doctor have to say
to me? Man, I've *had* my operation,
right?

Silence, and that's the worst answer there can be. Eberle can't meet Brian's look. After a beat, Brian looks over slowly to Gale.

BRIAN

Talk to me, Magic . . .

Gale discovers his voice after a second, but it emerges with anguish.

GALE

The tests show—there's more
of the tumor than they thought,
Pic. They have to operate again . . .

Once more, Eberle, seeking nothing more than escape, steps forward, holding out the surgical consent and a fountain pen.

EBERLE

So, if you'll just sign the
consent, Mr. . . .

BRIAN

(*turning away*)
No!

EBERLE

But putting this off won't be . . .

BRIAN

Are you deaf? I said *no*, damnit!

EBERLE

Mr. Sayers—can't you talk to
your friend?

Brian has moved to the window, shoulders hunched as if gathering himself for a blow of enormous force; but it's too late, the blow has been delivered already. Gale looks at him, then turns to Eberle.

GALE

No, Mr. Eberle, I think I'd
rather talk to *you.*

EBERLE

But . . .

GALE

Brian is a professional athlete,
Mr. Eberle. And a professional
gets into a habit after awhile. He
gets himself ready for a game
mentally as well as physically.
Because he knows those two things
are all tied up together. And
there's a clock going inside him,
so that when the game starts, he's
one hundred percent mentally and physically.
And what Pic is saying to you now,
is that you're scheduling this game
before he can get ready. Couldn't
it wait until over the weekend?

FULL SHOT

EBERLE

Well, yes, it *could*, but . . .

GALE

Then *let* it.

EBERLE

(*a beat, looks to Brian*)
First thing Monday morning, Mr.
Piccolo.

BRIAN

Okay.

EBERLE

I'll see you then.

Eberle strides stiffly to the door and steps out, smoothing his ruffled dignity as he goes. Gale looks back to Brian, who continues to gaze out the window. A beat, as Brian strains to salvage some control.

> BRIAN
>
> Thanks, Gale . . .

> GALE
>
> No sweat.

> BRIAN
>
> Thought you were the guy who
> didn't talk very well.

> GALE
>
> Well—I roomed with an Italian;
> you know how they are.

Brian turns away from the window. He moves back to the game board, idly scanning the setup. A beat, then a small smile appears on his face.

> BRIAN
>
> Guess what? I scored a touchdown.

We hold on Brian.

CUT TO BLACK OVER FOLLOWING:

> NURSE #1's VOICE
>
> Good morning, Mr. Piccolo. Time
> to wake up now.

FADE IN

MEDIUM SHOT—NURSE #1

She is looking into lens, smiling Cheshirely, a hypodermic needle in hand.

NURSE #1

I'm going to give you a little shot
to help you relax, Mr. Piccolo.
You'll be going up to the operating
room in about an hour.

BRIAN (*Offstage*)

My wife here?

NURSE #1

You'll see her when you come down,
Mr. Piccolo. Now, this won't
hurt a bit.

BRIAN (*Offstage*)

Yes—you're being very brave about
it all.

DIRECT CUT TO:

INTERIOR—OPERATING ROOM—DAY—UP
ANGLE

A Doctor, masked and gowned, leans into the lens,
arms held up away from his body.

DOCTOR

Mr. Piccolo—we're going to
put you to sleep now . . .

BRIAN (*Offstage*)

That's the—worst—choice of words
—I ever heard in my life . . .

As we start a slow fade to black, we begin to hear the
sound of applause, growing louder and louder with
each second. Then, in utter darkness:

M.C. (*Offstage*)
Gale Sayers!!!

CUT TO:

INTERIOR—BANQUET HALL—NIGHT—
TIGHT ON GALE

Dressed in a tuxedo, Gale starts as he becomes aware of the explosion of sounds being directed at him. Other men at his table poke Gale, all laughing as they urge him to his feet. Startled, he rises and the camera pans him as he is almost passed along from table to table by the others present.

THE DAIS

Gale smiles, still at a loss, and moves toward the toastmaster, who is holding out a large trophy to him. As Gale accepts the trophy with a muttered thank you the applause builds once more, a tidal wave of noise from the darkness. Gale looks down at the inscription on the trophy.

INSERT—THE INSCRIPTION

It reads: George S. Halas Award—Most Courageous Player—to Gale Sayers.

TIGHT ON GALE

He looks out, nodding acknowledgment to the applause. Slowly it starts to trail off, then dies. A moment of throat clearings, chairs shifting into better positions. When it is absolutely still, Gale begins to speak, leaning in to the microphone, his voice echoing slightly.

GALE

I'd like to say a few words about
a guy I know—a friend of mine.
His name is Brian Piccolo and he
has the heart of a giant—and
that rare form of courage that
allows him to kid himself and
his opponent—cancer. He has
the mental attitude that makes
me proud to have a friend who
spells out courage twenty-four
hours a day, every day of his
life.

Gale takes a sip of water from the glass next to the
podium.

GALE

You flatter me by giving me this
award—but I tell you here and
now I accept it for Brian Piccolo.
Brian Piccolo is the man of courage
who should receive the George S.
Halas Award. It is mine tonight;
it is Brian Piccolo's tomorrow.

Not a sound out there. Gale clutches the award tightly
and his eyes sparkle with tears. No attempt is made
to hide those tears.

GALE

I love Brian Piccolo—and I'd like
all of you to love him, too. And,
tonight—when you hit your knees . . .

(*beat*)
Please ask God to love him . . .

Gale steps quickly out of the spotlight. We hold on the empty circle for several seconds before the sound comes. First, one or two people, then more, and swiftly an avalanche of thunder.

DIRECT CUT TO:

INTERIOR—BRIAN'S HOSPITAL ROOM—DAY— ON BRIAN

Joy places the phone on the pillow next to him. When the angle widens, we see Linda is also present. There is an IV stand next to the bed, a tank of oxygen in the corner. Brian's face is drawn, the flesh pallid and shiny. We intercut the conversation with Gale in his hotel room.

BRIAN

Hi, Magic . . .

GALE

How are you, Pic?

BRIAN

Oh, hangin' in there . . .
(*beat*)
Heard what you did at the banquet.
If you were here, I'd kiss you . . .

GALE

Glad I'm not there, then.

BRIAN

Hey, Gale? They said you gave me
a pint of blood. Is that true?

GALE

Yeah.

BRIAN

That explains it, then.

GALE

Explains what?

BRIAN

I've had this craving for chitlins
all day.

Gale smiles on the other end.

GALE

I'll be in tomorrow morning, man.
I'll see you then.

BRIAN

Yeah—I ain't going nowhere ...

Joy takes the phone and hands it to Linda, who takes
the receiver to the window where the cradle is
located. Camera closes on Linda as she looks back to
Brian and Joy, now offstage. Linda raises the phone
to her ear.

LINDA

Gale?

GALE

How is he, Linda? *Really?*

LINDA

(*soft, yet urgently*)
Hurry. Gale—please hurry.

DIRECT CUT TO:

INTERIOR—BRIAN'S ROOM—NIGHT—ON ED McCASKEY

He is seated in a chair by the door, a continuous caressing of rosary beads sliding through his fingers. The room is striped with sunlight from the partially closed venetian blinds. The door is opened and Gale and Linda come in. Brian's eyes are closed, and his frame seems small beneath the blankets. Joy bends to him as Gale moves quietly to the other side of the bed, Linda holding by the door.

JOY

Brian—Gale's here.

CLOSER ANGLE—GALE AND BRIAN

Brian's hand comes up from the sheet in greeting. Gale takes the hand in his. His eyelids are fighting a terrible weight and his words come slowly, breath on a ration.

BRIAN

Hello, Black Magic.

GALE

You are so bad—a racist, that's all you are. Bigot from head to toe.

BRIAN

Believe it, man.

GALE

(*after a beat*)
How's it going, Pic?

BRIAN

It's fourth and eight, man—but
they won't let me punt.

GALE

Go for it, then.

BRIAN

I'm trying, Gale—Jesus God,
how I'm trying . . .

Suddenly an agonizing spasm rips through his frame as a thousand screaming nerve ends are consumed by the cellular inferno. Brian's head snaps back, his hand convulses on Gale's. Tears spilling down her cheeks, Joy leans close to her husband.

Seconds go by, terrible instants of impotent love. Then, slowly, Brian's body relaxes and his head touches the pillow. Joy blots the perspiration from his brow. His eye goes to Gale.

BRIAN

Remember that first year . . . couldn't
get a word out of you . . .

GALE

Couldn't get you to shut up . . .

BRIAN

Remember how you got me with those
mashed potatoes . . .

GALE

You deserved it—the way you sang
that dumb fight song—twice, you

did it—at camp, and that time
down in my basement . . .
  (*beat*)
And that 32 trap play—remember
that?

BRIAN

Yeah. How could I forget?

There is a pause. Brian's look turns reflective. He
smiles.

BRIAN

You taught me a lot about running,
Gale. I appreciate it.

GALE

I wouldn't be running if I hadn't
had you pushin' me—helping me . . .

BRIAN

I'll get you next training camp . . .

GALE

I'll be waiting . . .

BRIAN

Yeah . . .
  (*a sigh*)
Gale, I'm feeling kind of punk . . .
I think I'll sack out for a while,
okay?

GALE

Sure thing.

ANGLE TO THEIR HANDS

Gale gently lets go of Brian's hand, which falls limply back onto the sheet. Gale's hand rests on the other for a beat, then he moves away.

FULL SHOT

The nun opens the door for Gale and Linda. He stops, looking back, his voice choked. Linda holds his arm tightly, her eyes shine with tears held in check.

GALE
See you tomorrow, Pic . . .

TIGHT ON BRIAN

He turns his head toward Gale, brings his gaze into focus. He lifts the hand closest to the door and gives a "thumbs-up."

BRIAN
If you say so . . .

Offstage, the sound of the door is quietly closed. Brian pulls Joy close to him, his arms about her. His eyes close, the rate of his breathing slackens. Joy's lips are close to Brian's ear.

JOY
I love you, Brian—I love you. . . .

Brian forces his eyes open and looks at her for a long beat. He finds one final smile.

BRIAN
Who'd believe it, Joy—who'd
ever believe it . . .

And they are close for the last time. This stillness will endure.

DISSOLVE TO:

EXTERIOR—HOSPITAL PARKING LOT—NIGHT —ON GALE AND LINDA

Arm in arm they move slowly along the line of cars in the parking lot until they come to their own. Gale opens the door on Linda's side and helps her in. As he closes the door, he looks to the hospital.

HIS POINT OF VIEW—HOSPITAL WINDOW

Zooming in on McCaskey in Brian's room. He slowly closes the blinds.

TIGHT ON GALE

He gazes at the hospital.

> NARRATOR (*Voice Over*)
> Brian Piccolo died of cancer at
> the age of twenty-six. He left
> a wife and three daughters.

Superimpose over the close shot of Gale Sayers in the parking lot, footage from the footrace between Gale and Brian, ending with slow motion of their contest that freezes on a tight shot of Brian.

> NARRATOR (*Voice Over*)
> He also left a great many loving
> friends who miss him and think
> of him often. But, when they think
> of him, it's not how he died that

they remember but, rather, how he
lived . . .
   (*beat*)
How he *did* live . . .

And as Gale moves around to his side of the car and starts to get in, the image of Brian takes precedence, smiling and full of hell and life. A good face to study for a moment or two.

FADE OUT

DISCOVER THE DRAMA OF LIFE IN THE LIFE OF DRAMA

☐	26366	THE ACTOR'S SCENEBOOK by M. Schulman & E. Mekler	$4.95
☐	25434	FILM SCENES FOR ACTORS Joshua Karton	$4.95
☐	21118	CYRANO DE BERGERAC Elmond Rostand	$1.75
☐	21165	FOUR GREAT PLAYS Henrik Ibsen	$2.50
☐	26212	FOR COLORED GIRLS WHO HAVE CONSIDERED SUICIDE WHEN THE RAINBOW IS ENUF Ntozake Shange	$3.50
☐	25844	MODERN AMERICAN SCENES FOR STUDENT ACTORS Wynn Handman	$4.50
☐	34330	SAM SHEPHERD: SEVEN PLAYS Sam Shepard (A Large Format)	$7.95
☐	23417	THE NIGHT THOREAU SPENT IN JAIL Jerome Lawrence and Robert E. Lee	$2.95
☐	24072	BRIAN'S SONG William Blinn	$2.50
☐	24741	THE EFFECTS OF GAMMA RAYS ON MAN-IN-THE-MOON MARIGOLDS Paul Zindel	$2.95
☐	25435	INHERIT THE WIND Lawrence & Lee	$2.75
☐	21219	EURIPIDES Ten Plays Moses Hadas, ed.	$3.50
☐	24778	THE MIRACLE WORKER William Gibson	$2.95

Buy them at your local bookstore or use this convenient coupon for ordering.

Bantam Books, Inc., Dept. EDH, 414 East Golf Road, Des Plaines, Ill. 60016

Please send me the books I have checked above. I am enclosing $_____
(please add $1.50 to cover postage and handling). Send check or money order
—no cash or C.O.D.'s please.

Mr/Mrs/Miss _____

Address _____

City _____ State/Zip _____

EDH—9/86

Please allow four to six weeks for delivery. This offer expires 3/87.

BANTAM
SHOP-AT-HOME
C·A·T·A·L·O·G

Special Offer
Buy a Bantam Book
for only 50¢.

Now you can have Bantam's catalog filled with hundreds of titles plus take advantage of our unique and exciting bonus book offer. A special offer which gives you the opportunity to purchase a Bantam book for only 50¢. Here's how!

By ordering any five books at the regular price per order, you can also choose any other single book listed (up to a $4.95 value) for just 50¢. Some restrictions do apply, but for further details why not send for Bantam's catalog of titles today!

Just send us your name and address and we will send you a catalog!

BANTAM BOOKS, INC.
P.O. Box 1006, South Holland, Ill. 60473

Mr./Mrs./Miss/Ms. _____
(please print)

Address _____

City _____ State _____ Zip _____

FC(A)—11/88

Please allow four to six weeks for delivery.